THE Book of Altars and Sacred Spaces

THE Book of Altars and Sacred Spaces

How to Create Magical Spaces in Your
Home for Ritual and Intention

ANJOU KIERNAN

FAIR WINDS

Inspiring | Educating | Creating | Entertaining

Brimming with creative inspiration, how-to projects, and useful information to enrich your everyday life, Quarto Knows is a favorite destination for those pursuing their interests and passions. Visit our site and dig deeper with our books into your area of interest: Quarto Creates, Quarto Cooks, Quarto Homes, Quarto Lives, Quarto Drives, Quarto Explores, Quarto Gifts, or Quarto Kids.

24 23 22 21 20   1 2 3 4 5

ISBN: 978-1-59233-944-0

Digital edition published in 2020

Library of Congress Control Number: 2020932767

Cover Design: Tanya Jacobson, crsld.co
Page Layout: Megan Jones Design
Photography: Anjou Kiernan
Illustration: Anjou Kiernan page 9, all others Shutterstock
Printed in China

TO ALL THOSE WHO SEEK TO UNEARTH
THE VERY ROOTS OF OUR MAGICK.

CONTENTS

INTRODUCTION

In this world, simple moments of mindfulness can create explosions of magick. Finding space for these moments—*sacred space*—requires conscious curation of our environment into nooks of ritual and ceremony. Sacred space nurtures our body, feeds our mind, and coaxes energy from our spirit. It dredges up our deepest fears and delves into our darkest desires. It is where we work our magick, unearth our personal truth, and foster our relationship with nature. Sacred space can mean many things to many people, but it is first and foremost a place where we feel safe to connect with ourselves and the world around us.

In witchcraft, we might reserve sacred space for ritual and spellcasting and create a dedicated area that houses all our magickal tools. Or we might seek sacredness wherever the wind blows, like a nomad setting up camp for the night. Sacred space can be highly personal or serve a community or coven; think of the temples, churches, and circles where mindful work is often performed. But no matter its form or location, the underlying purpose of sacred space is to bridge the gap between the physical and the metaphysical as it weaves our energies together with the universe.

magickal work. In many theistic religions, altars are raised structures reserved for sacred rites and sacrifices to gods and goddesses. But in modern pagan practices, altars function not only as powerful places for ritual and spellcasting, but as foundations for offerings of gratitude, symbols of the season, shrines to deities or nature spirits, and places to capture intentional stillness and quiet focus. You may choose to have a single altar in your home that caters to your rituals, or you may create these pockets of magick throughout your environment. Your mindful journey through the world is yours to curate.

Altars

Within a sacred space, the heart of the mindful practice—the altar—beats. It fills up with the energies that we pour into it, like a chalice receiving wine. This concentrated energy makes an altar a powerful place to do

The Wheel of the Year

As you travel along your journey, you will notice that your magick naturally follows the turn of the seasons. Each of these turns corresponds to a solar event that is honored by a holiday (also known as a "sabbat" in Wicca)

on the pagan calendar, the Wheel of the Year. The Wheel of the Year consists of eight holidays or festivals that mark transitional times of the year. Beginning with Midwinter on the longest night of the year, the Wheel slowly spins as the barren winter land blossoms into spring and bursts forth into the harvests of summer and fall. Although each holiday is celebrated in its own right, there are three general truths to keep in mind when planning seasonal sacred spaces to correspond with them: The solstices (the longest and shortest days of the year) bid farewell to one half of the year and welcome the next; the equinoxes (when night and day are of equal length) honor the balance of light and dark; and the cross-quarter days (the midway points of each of the four seasons) prepare for transition.

The holidays on the Wheel of the Year celebrate traditions that have been adapted from the pagan cultures of ancient Europe. These festivals often called for great feasts, village bonfires, or other large gatherings to honor the cultivation of community for survival and success throughout the year. The pagans of yesteryear were deeply tied to the land, and many of the festivals' enduring traditions hark back to ancient farming practices. They were opportunities to give gratitude to the Sun, as well as to cultural deities and folk figures thought to influence seasonal patterns. Though these traditions may not necessarily be relevant to your life or region, they have symbolic purpose that can bring meaning and intention to your seasonal altars and sacred space.

In preparing your holiday celebrations, remember that your traditions might vary based on your own regional observations. The Wheel's seasonal timing drew mostly from the climate of northern Europe, which may not reflect your own region's occurrences. Even within ancient pagan societies, timing differed based on location. Ireland has historically only had two seasons: winter, which began at Samhain, and summer, which began at Beltane. This is why, even across many countries and practices, we consider Samhain and Beltane to be the transitional, liminal times of the year.

Setting Up Your Sacred Space

As you follow the Wheel of the Year, you will want to create spaces in which to honor the traditions and transitions that attune your magick to the pulse of nature. These spaces will flux with your own needs and the needs of the world around you. Curating your environment into a mindful journey through the seasons will be largely influenced by this symbiotic relationship. It will require you to consider several factors, especially intention, location, and foundation.

INTENTION

The first step in creating a sacred space is deciding on your intention. Where are you on the Wheel of the Year? What seasonal traditions or symbols speak to you and your individual practice? Would you like to express gratitude for the abundance of the season or perhaps honor a deity or nature spirit? Or would you like to plan a ritual based on a quality that the season brings, such as growth or cleansing? Perhaps you want to take advantage of the timing to perform pagan traditions such as handfasting or fertility spells. In magick, intention is everything, and your sacred space will be that much more effective if it captures the proper energy. Visualize it, meditate on it, write it down, and journal about it. Then, and only then, begin to energize your intention.

LOCATION

Magickal spaces can exist anywhere, but knowing where *you* work your magick best is the key to making your sacred space work for *you*. Many times, your intention will help guide you to the best location. For instance, an offering to the faeries would be best placed where they dwell—outdoors, near a garden or forest entrance. And a confidence shrine might be best suited to a private space with a mirror, such as a bathroom or bedroom vanity. If heading outdoors, tree hollows, forest glades, water edges, grottos (whether natural or artificial), and other natural formations are sometimes the most powerful places to make magick and can easily house even temporary sacred spaces. In fact, a serene and tucked-away forest glade has become my favorite place to meditate or call upon the elements. Weather, too, will be an inescapable factor when choosing a location—it might prove a bit difficult to have a balefire in a thunderstorm! No matter your surroundings or your ability to access nature, most sacred spaces in this book can be modified so that they are just as effective indoors. Simply focus on the symbolism—the balefire we mentioned could be contained in a jar candle and decorated with stones or sticks around the base. The intention and focus are still there, but your "balefire" is now fit for an indoor space.

Once you have decided whether your sacred space will be out in nature or in the privacy of your own home, it is time to delve into the nuances of its location. Consider not only your intention, but how much space you will need, the permanence and privacy requirements of the space, whether it should be in view of the Moon or Sun, and the direction it should face. Because the Wheel of the Year is based on solar events, it is a good idea to have the altar or sacred space situated in the East with the rising Sun, unless you are calling upon a particular element or honoring the planetary ruler of a deity or nature spirit. You may also choose to face the altar in the cardinal direction of the ruling element of the season.

FOUNDATION

The foundation of your altar or other sacred space will be largely influenced by its location. If outdoors, a tree stump, concrete pedestal, table, flat stone, balcony shelf, or garden ledge could make for a sturdy place to house your altar. For these spaces, I like to use decorative trays or bowls to keep everything in place—you would be surprised how far wind and wildlife can scatter your perfectly composed altar. When indoors, you have an array of options available to you; almost any surface can be made into a sacred space. Fireplace mantles, bookshelves, tables, countertops, cutting boards, bedside trays, entryway benches, vanities, and the rim of a bathtub can accommodate altars. If you plan to travel with your altar, you can even squeeze its components into a pocket-sized tin.

Common Altar Items

As the Wheel of the Year turns, your altar items will flux with the seasons and the traditions that correspond with them. However, some magickal tools find their ways to many sacred spaces. As you arrange your altars, keep in mind that elemental tools should be placed at their respective cardinal directions to call the energy of the elements to your sacred space.

ALTAR CLOTH: An altar cloth is a natural fiber or decorative cloth that protects the surface of your altar. Its colors can be chosen based on the holiday or season, and it can be painted or embroidered with symbolic images to draw specific energy to the altar.

BLADE: A blade is a utility knife used to ceremoniously cut herbs, cut twine, and carve symbols into candles. It is often curved similar to a sickle, scythe, or Wiccan Boline.

CANDLE: A candle is symbolic of the Fire element and should be placed in the South when used in an elemental aspect. Colors are chosen for symbolic purposes (for example, red for love or black for protection) or according to the colors of the holiday or season. Candles can be dressed with herbs and oils and carved with symbols. They are also used to burn intentions and can be spells in and of themselves.

CANDLE COLOR ASSOCIATIONS

RED (FIRE ELEMENT):
Love, passion, stimulation

BLUE (WATER ELEMENT):
Meditation, communication, emotions

YELLOW (AIR ELEMENT):
Joy, happiness, success

GREEN (EARTH ELEMENT):
Wealth, prosperity, luck

PURPLE (SPIRIT ELEMENT):
Divination, spiritual growth

WHITE: Peace, purity, harmony

BLACK: Protection, grounding

CHALICE OR CAULDRON: A chalice or cauldron is symbolic of the Water element and should be placed in the West when used in an elemental aspect. It can be filled with elemental water, herbal decoctions, wine, beer, mead, distillations, infused oils, honey, soil, crystals, bones, salt, or other elements reflective of the season or holiday.

CORD: A cord is a natural-fiber thin rope, twine, or yarn used for wrapping herbs or binding spells.

CRYSTAL: A crystal is a gem, stone, or fossil used to impart or direct vibrational energy to your intention. It should be cleansed and charged with moonlight, sunlight, water, salt, herbal smoke, or other crystals before each ritual. Quartz, citrine, and amethyst clusters as well as selenite slabs can be used to cleanse and charge other crystals and magickal tools. Note that some crystals are more delicate than others and should not be cleansed in water, sunlight, or salt.

DIVINATION TOOL: A divination tool is used to peer into the unknown and gain wisdom for self-empowerment or rituals. It could be, for example, a dowsing pendulum, tarot or oracle deck, crystal ball, scrying mirror, set of runes, teacup for tasseomancy, or set of casting bones.

COMMON ALTAR CRYSTALS AND THEIR ASSOCIATIONS

AMETHYST: Serenity, clarity, spirituality

BLACK TOURMALINE: Protection, transformation, grounding

CARNELIAN: Stimulation, encouragement, energy

CITRINE: Manifestation, healing, revitalization

CLEAR QUARTZ: Amplification, cleansing, healing

FLUORITE: Harmony, balance, spirituality

LABRADORITE: Transformation, mysticism, stimulation of psychic abilities

MOONSTONE: Emotional balance, intuition, receptivity

ROSE QUARTZ: Healing, love, soothing

SELENITE: Cleansing, light-bringing, transformation

DOLLY, FIGURINE, OR STATUE:
A dolly is a symbolic representation of a deity or other venerated figure (such as nature spirits or celestial bodies). It is used in sympathetic magick and is often appeased with offerings of gratitude to call upon its energy. It may be constructed of straw, corn husk, clay, metal, wood, willow or apple tree twigs, or any other natural material that can be shaped.

FEATHER: Feathers are symbolic of the Air element and should be placed in the East when used in their elemental aspect. They can be used symbolically or to waft herbal smoke across a space for cleansing. Feathers should be found fallen or ethically sourced.

FIREPROOF VESSEL: A fireproof vessel, also called a burning pot, can be made of granite, soapstone, cast iron, or abalone and is used for ritually burning intentions, incense, or herbs.

HERBS AND INCENSE: Loose herbs or incense cones/sticks can be burned for cleansing or charging. Loose herbs are typically burned in a fireproof vessel on a disc of charcoal, but they can also be sprinkled around the space, used to dress a candle, cast into a fire, or infused into herbal sprays, waters, and intention or anointing oils.

INTENTION PAPER: Intention paper is used for what is known as *petition magick* to write down your wishes, goals, or intentions in ritual. You may use bay leaves, birch paper, parchment, or any natural fiber paper that is available to you. These are often burned in a fireproof vessel so that the ashes can be released as elemental magick or sown into the Earth.

SALT: Salt is symbolic of the Earth element and should be placed in the North when used in its elemental aspect. It is used for cleansing and protection from negative energy and can be sprinkled around the altar, in a circle around your sacred space, or along the thresholds of your space or home. Black salt is a powerful blend of dead sea salt and powdered wood ash (usually oak or ash) used to banish spirits or other negative energies.

WAND: A wand is a vibrational tool used to direct energy in a ritual. It is often created from sacred wood, copper, animal horns, or selenite or other crystals and can be carved with symbols or decorated with stones, crystals, and other natural elements.

CHAPTER 1

MIDWINTER

Northern Hemisphere: December 21; Southern Hemisphere: June 21

The solar year begins here on the solstice at Midwinter. The longest night of the year casts its shadow across the barren land as frigid temperatures and heavy snow fall in many northern regions. Those who brave winter's icy grip have now entered its most difficult stretch—the one that brings both physical and spiritual famine despite all that has been done to prepare. But with hardship comes hope. From here on out, the days will grow longer as the Earth begins to tilt back toward the Sun.

Prehistoric humans closely monitored the solar calendar, tracking the Sun's movement using monuments such as the Neolithic Newgrange burial mound in Ireland and Stonehenge in England. Even now, across many cultures all over the world, the promise of spring stokes hearth fires throughout the Midwinter festivals. These Pagan celebrations of light originate from the ancient belief that fire rites encourage the rebirth of the Sun, bringing renewal to homes and fields. Many ancient cultures celebrated the Winter Solstice accordingly: Druids welcomed the symbolic return of the legendary King Arthur during Alban Arthan. Romans celebrated Saturnalia, a holiday that honored Saturn, the god of agriculture and harvest. Egyptians welcomed the rebirth of the Sun god, Horus, who brought warmth to the crop fields. In

Scandinavia, the Norse drank ale and made sacrifices to the gods as Odin led the fierce winds and storm squalls of the spectral Wild Hunt across the sky.

During many of these festivals, it was customary to welcome the return of the light with great feasts and merrymaking. Although food would soon be scarce, Midwinter celebrations were a time for indulgence. The fruits of autumn harvests were prepared and the pastures were cleared, so meat was plentiful. By this time of year, wine and beer had fermented into potent brews, and cider had been pressed, bringing communities together over drink to sing and tell tales around roaring fires. Charitable acts and gift-giving, too, have been a traditional part of many Midwinter festivals as a way of sharing the abundance and good tidings of the holiday season.

YULE ALTAR

The Yule altar is a place to gather and share in the food, drinks, and festivities of the Yuletide season. It can be created on the dining table where the feast will take place or a sideboard table in the home's main room. Dress it in layers of altar cloths in rich emerald greens, ruby reds, and snow whites, and accent them with hints of gold and silver to represent the return of the light.

MAGICKAL CORRESPONDENCES OF YULE

ALTERNATIVE NAMES:
Christmastide (Christian), Saturnalia (Roman), Alban Arthan (Druid)

COLORS: Red, green, white, gold, silver

CRYSTALS: Ruby, garnet, emerald, bloodstone, diamond, clear quartz

DEITIES: Odin (Norse), Holly and Oak Kings (Celtic), Ra and Horus (Egyptian), Saturn (Roman)

ELEMENT: Earth

FLOWERS, HERBS, AND TREES:
Bay laurel, blessed thistle, bayberry, evergreens (cedar, holly, ivy, juniper, mistletoe, spruce, pine, fir), birch, oak, ash, cinnamon, nutmeg, clove, orange, frankincense, myrrh, wintergreen

FOODS: Mulled cider, wassail, oranges, figs, plums, ham, Yule log cake and fruit cakes, eggnog

SYMBOLS: Yule tree, Yule log, evergreen wreaths and boughs, pinecones, bells, wheels, lights

THEMES: Return of the light, rebirth of the Sun, cycle of life, ghosts, joy, peace, charity

Although modern Yule celebrations have evolved from many ancient pagan traditions from across Europe and beyond, most of what we have come to associate with the Midwinter holiday is derived from the practices of the ancient Germanic peoples. In fact, it is thought that the term *Yule* comes from the Old Norse word *hjól*, meaning "wheel." At the Winter Solstice, these ancient pagans welcomed the return of the Sun, a fiery wheel in the sky, as it rolled back toward the Earth, bringing warmth and vitality back to the fields and pastures. And so, in some neopagan traditions, it is customary to include prehistoric solar symbols such as the sunwheel or a Sun cross on the Yule altar. Incorporating other artifacts of the Sun—such as gold discs, plates or medallions, wreaths, artwork, or fiery colors including gold, yellow, orange, and red— is thought to encourage the return of the light and honor the incredible power that the Sun holds over all life on Earth.

Candles, too, call upon this energy in the form of the Fire element—a stimulating, life-giving property associated with the Sun. Lanterns, twinkle lights, tinsel, silver or white items, or even cutouts of stars can bring the promise of light to your Yule altar.

Druid orders celebrate Alban Arthan ("The Light of Arthur") in honor of the legendary King Arthur Pendragon, who is symbolically reborn as the Mabon (the "Son of Light" or "Sun Child") at the Winter Solstice. On this night, the Druids are said to have ceremoniously gathered mistletoe, a sacred evergreen that symbolizes immortality, from the oak trees on which it grew to heal certain afflictions. It is thought that this is where the traditional colors of Midwinter come from—the red of holly berries, the white of mistletoe berries, and the green of evergreen boughs. Incorporating these colors into your Yule altar in the form of candles, lights, bows, altar cloths, and vessels

Incorporating other artifacts of the Sun—such as gold discs, plates or medallions, wreaths, artwork, or fiery colors including gold, yellow, orange, and red—is thought to encourage the return of the light and honor the incredible power that the Sun holds over all life on Earth.

symbolizes the triumph of life through lean times.

In Celtic folklore, Yuletide is also the season to bid farewell to the Holly King, who rules the darker half of the year, and welcome the Oak King, who has finally defeated his rival and brought light back to the land. It is customary to honor both kings at this time by adorning the Yule altar with evergreens such as mistletoe, holly, pine, fir, ivy, and pinecones as well as oak leaves and acorns. The prick of a holly leaf is also said to provide protection against meddling spirits. Winding it around your altar ensures that only positive energies enter your space.

The Yule tree, a precursor to the Christmas tree, was a symbol of everlasting life in many ancient pagan Midwinter customs. The Druids decorated the holly tree with symbols of dreams and wishes for the New Year, while the Scandinavians brought their tree indoors to provide a warm place for the nature spirits to dwell during the winter cold. There, they hung small gifts or symbols of the hunt from its branches. You can incorporate a small tabletop tree or wreath into the Yule altar, so you can hang intentions or gifts on its branches to please the nature spirits in hopes that they will return the blessing come spring.

The Anglo-Saxon tradition of wassailing could mean blessing fruit trees by pouring wine or cider on them to bring prosperity and fruitfulness to the New Year. It could also refer to hot spiced cider that is sipped from a shared bowl in exchange for gifts while merrymaking from house to house. Either way, this tradition is a wonderful addition to neo-pagan Yule celebrations. Incorporating dried apple slices, a wassail bowl, mulled wine, a drinking horn, or sheet music of classic wassailing or caroling songs into the Yule altar can bring back this ancient custom and make your altar a festive place of communing and merriment.

Baking, too, is a favorite pastime of Yule. Including sacred spices such as nutmeg, clove, and cinnamon in the Yule altar is an excellent way to connect with the season. A potpourri pot, incense burner, or even a dusting of spices on the altar cloth can accompany seasonal offerings such as cookies, fruit cake, or a traditional Yule log cake. Make pomander balls, a creation of medieval herbalists, by piercing oranges with a design of cloves and dusting them in spices. They can be hung around the Yule altar to freshen the air and protect the home from negative energies.

If deities are in your practice, you can include symbolic figures of Saturn (Roman), Ra and Horus (Egyptian Sun gods), the Holly King (Druid), Brigid (Celtic bearer of the flame), Lugh and Eriu (Celtic God of Light and Earth Mother), or the Nordic Yule-Beings of Odin and Frigg and their sons Baldr, Hodr, and Thor (biological son of the Earth Mother). Because Yule is a transitional time when the darkness falls to light, nature spirits and specters are thought to freely roam the land. Making offerings to or incorporating figures of faeries, elves, trolls, and ghosts can invite their presence into your celebration and ensure their blessings. The ringing of a silver bell is thought to invite the light-bringing spirits into your space and drive away the evil lurking in the dark.

WINTER SOLSTICE SPIRAL

Set intentions for each month of the new year.

Materials

13 white candles
(taper, pillar, or tealights)

Evergreen branches

Sprigs of holly and mistletoe

The Winter Solstice marks a warm welcome to the return of the light. As your region of the Earth begins to tilt back toward the Sun after it reaches the solstice, the days will grow longer and the nights shorter. Since prehistoric times, the Winter Solstice has been celebrated as the rebirth of the Sun and a time for transformation. Farming communities relied on the Sun for their crops' growth, and the solstice brought with it the promise of a renewed harvest season. As we emerge from our long winter slumber, we use the standstill of the solstice as a time of reflection, leaving behind the things that no longer serve us and making room for the growth and new beginnings that the return of the light will bring.

This transformation is the focus of a Solstice Spiral, a sacred tradition with roots in the Waldorf education system that symbolizes the journey we take from darkness to light. The spiral itself is crafted of evergreen branches and twelve evenly spaced candles to represent each month of the coming year with a central candle that represents our inner light. Intentions can be set for each candle. As we physically walk the labyrinth during the darkest night, we light the candles along the path with the flame of the center candle, kindling each intention with our inner light and shining light on our shadow self, thereby empowering our journey throughout the coming year. The Solstice Spiral is best set up in an open outdoor space. It can even be a community space, if you would like to allow others to join you in the journey to the deeper self. If you do not have an adequate outdoor space, feel free to create a small-scale spiral with tealight candles, lighting each as if you were walking amongst them.

If deities are in your practice, you may also honor the rebirth of the Sun by placing symbols or figures of Sun and fertility gods and goddesses along the spiral. In Celtic-based traditions, it is customary to include sprigs of holly and mistletoe to honor the Holly and Oak Kings.

YULE LOG

Symbolically welcome the return of the Sun.

Materials

Green altar cloth

Log

Drill or carving knife

Spices such as nutmeg, clove, and cinnamon

Flour

Evergreen branches and berries

3 twenty-four-hour taper candles in red, green, and white

Bay leaves

Marker or pen

The Yule log harks back to the traditions of the early Germanic peoples of ancient Europe. In the home's hearth, a whole tree was burned for the twelve days between the solstice and the New Year. The tree was carefully selected and ceremoniously brought into the home so that it might be cleansed and blessed. At the end of the Yuletide season, a piece of coal was set aside for kindling the next year's log, and the ashes were kept in the home for protection against misfortune. Come spring, the ashes would be sown into the fields to bless and fertilize the seeds. As hearths became smaller and home heating more efficient, the feasibility of this ancient Yule log tradition dwindled. In modern pagan and Christian festivities, the Yule log is often represented by a birch log that has been made into a candle centerpiece.

Whether you display your Yule log as a festive table centerpiece, clear a spot for it on the fireplace mantle, or place it on a rack in the hearth, this tradition can impart millennia of symbolism into your holiday celebrations. If laying an altar cloth, you may choose green to represent the immortality of evergreens. For the log itself, you can use any of the sacred woods such as birch, pine, or cherry. Once you have physically and ritually cleansed the log, drill or carve three evenly spaced holes that are large enough to accommodate taper candles on the top. Then dust the log in nutmeg, clove, cinnamon, and flour and dress it with evergreens and berries. Place three candles in the Druidic colors of red, green, and white in the holes. You may include bay leaves and a marker or pen so that you and your guests can write wishes for the new year on the leaves. If you celebrate Yule in solitude, you could use twelve bay leaves to represent an intention for each month of the year to come.

WASSAILING DRINK CART

Encourage good cheer, community, and fertility of the land.

Materials

Drink cart or small table

Candles in gold, silver, red, or green

Festive greenery and fruits such as evergreen boughs, holly, ivy, apples, cranberries, and pomander balls (see page 23)

Wassail bowl (a wooden, copper, tin, pewter, or ceramic bowl or even a crockpot)

Punch cups and a ladle

Wassail: apple cider, ale, or wine mulled using a recipe of your choice

Wassailing card or sheet music

Like many Christmas traditions, caroling has its origins in paganism. Wassailing dates back to pre-Christian Europe, when farmers in the apple-producing regions of England often spent the Twelfth Night of the Yuletide season blessing the trees with cider. As the custom evolved, wassailing began to take on many of its modern characteristics: From the gathering of drunken tenants at their Lord's manor house in demand of holiday treats, to the door-to-door blessings and spirited singing with wassail in hand, the tradition of wassailing has in many ways shaped the modern practice of caroling. In fact, the words of popular Christmas carols still carry some of the early wassailer's demands: *"Oh, bring us some figgy pudding . . . We won't go until we've got some . . . So bring some out here!"*

Wassail is a tradition best served on a drink cart dressed with evergreen boughs, apples, cranberries, holly, ivy, pomander balls, and candles in gold, silver, or the Druidic colors of Yule. Use the wassail bowl to keep the wassail warm throughout the evening. Fill the bowl with wassail made using a recipe of your choice—perhaps a warmed and spiced cider, ale, or wine mulled with sugar, nutmeg, cinnamon, ginger, and cloves. Bitters, oranges, eggs, and liquor such as rum or brandy are sometimes added. Traditionally, wassail is also topped with toast or cakes to soak up the cider that can then be shared as good tidings with friends and family. Unless you prefer a communal bowl, you may also want to include punch cups and a ladle. In front of the bowl, place a card with the following wassailing song from the Middle Ages to encourage everyone who takes a drink to spread the good cheer of wassail.

Wassail, wassail all over the town
Our toast it is white and our ale it
* is brown;*
Our bowl it is made of the good
* maple tree;*
With the wassailing bowl we'll drink
* unto thee.*

RETURN OF THE LIGHT JAR

Bring light into the darkest hour.

Materials

Mason jar with solar-powered light lid

Crystals such as clear quartz, smoky quartz, rose quartz, amethyst, citrine, sunstone, and carnelian

Gold or silver round tray

Dried summer flowers and herbs such as sunflower petals, calendula, St. John's wort, and dandelions

Sunflower oil (optional)

The longest night brings with it the promise of the return of the light. For those who rely on the land for survival, the arrival of the solstice means that the physical hardships of winter will soon come to an end. And for those whose spirits have suffered at the hands of their shadow selves, the solstice is a beacon of hope that the heavy blanket of darkness will soon lift. The "winter blues" can cause lethargy and low mood and can drain our wells of magick. Throughout history, light has been used to heal not only physical ailments but psychological and spiritual ones as well. By including candles, hearth fires, lanterns, and twinkle lights in our sacred space, we can bathe in the warmth, joy, and creativity they evoke on even the darkest of days.

This portable altar is meant to be a small beacon of hope that can be transported from room to room. Fill the bottom of a mason jar with crystals that cleanse or transmute negative energy (such as clear quartz, smoky quartz, and amethyst), vibrate gentle healing energies (such as rose quartz), or stimulate solar energies (such as citrine, sunstone, and carnelian). If you like, assign each crystal a hope or wish for the year to come. Screw a solar-powered light lid onto the top of the jar and place the jar on a round gold or silver tray. In a sunny spot outdoors, allow the jar to soak up the rays of the winter Sun throughout the day. Surround the jar with dried flowers and herbs from the summer such as sunflower petals, calendula, St. John's wort, and dandelions. At dusk, move the jar and tray with the sunlight-soaked herbs and flowers to a table or shelf in a darkened room. Use this as a meditation space and bright spot in your life during the long nights. Burn the loose herbs as incense or infuse them into sunflower oil to craft a recharging and awakening anointing oil.

SPIRITED READING NOOK

Share spectral tales 'round the yule fire.

Materials

Comfortable chair

Blankets or silks in rich, festive colors— emerald greens, deep burgundies and plums, iridescent golds and silvers, and creamy ivories

Dim light, candles, or twinkle lights and pegs to hang them on

Candle quartz crystal

Several floor pillows or plush ottomans (optional)

Book shelving system (optional)

Books containing stories of Yuletide traditions, holiday spirits, and other spectral tales

The tradition of sharing spooky stories 'round the Yule log dates back to the Midwinter celebrations of the Germanic peoples. Before the invention of electricity and central heat, the ancient pagans took comfort in the hearth fire. Storytelling was not only a way to pass the time, but to bond with family—alive and dead—and to bring life to the dark gods and goddesses so that their blessings might be gained. These tales often explored the cycle of death and rebirth by focusing on ghostly visitors, meddling faeries, or the deities' deliverance of great blessings or curses on mankind. Upon the Christianization of Yule, and later through the beloved works of Charles Dickens, the pagan art of Midwinter ghost stories became an integral tradition of Christmastide.

With the advent of film and television, the Yuletide tradition of oral storytelling has become a lost art. By introducing a festive reading nook into your home, you can help to reintegrate this practice into the Midwinter holiday. Choose a corner that has a comfortable chair on which to sit and read. Drape layers of blankets or silks on the chair. To impart a magickal glow on the nook, choose a dim light, candles, or twinkle lights hung from pegs on the walls. With its gentle radiance, candle quartz is a wonderful crystal ally for this space and can be placed on a small table or stack of books. If you are creating a community nook, include several floor pillows or ottomans for listeners to sit comfortably on. Then, begin to construct your library. Create a shelving system or simply stack a few books in the space. Select stories that tell of Yuletide traditions, holiday spirits, and other spectral tales, or infuse your favorite ghostly legends with the Yuletide spirit. You might even play a Yuletide version of "Pass the Story" with your circle or family wherein each person contributes a sentence until the ghostly tale has reached its natural, or *supernatural,* conclusion.

CHAPTER 2

IMBOLC

Northern Hemisphere: February 1; Southern Hemisphere: August 1

Although the solstice snow still lingers in some northern regions, the Celtic holiday of Imbolc, a cross-quarter day between the Winter Solstice and the Spring Equinox, is the time to prepare for the rebirth of the land. As the soil softens and the winds warm, the quickening of the earth is imminent. Farmers ready their agricultural tools in preparation for sowing the fields and stocking the pastures with newborn farm animals. In Old Irish, the term *imbolc* means "in the belly"—a reminder that the season brings fertile ground and the birth of lambing season. Imbolc is one of four major fire festivals on the Irish calendar and the official beginning of Spring in Ireland. On the mornings of both Imbolc and the other Celtic cross-quarter holiday, Samhain, a chamber in the Neolithic Mound of the Hostages on the Hill of Tara fills with light, signifying the halfway point to the equinox in each half of the year.

Also known as Brigid's Day, Imbolc celebrates the pagan hearth goddess Brigid, whose triple aspects of healing, smithcraft, and poetry are united by the fire of her sacred flames. Although Brigid has pre-Christian origins in Ireland, she was adopted into Christianity during the medieval conversion of the country. She became Saint Brigid of Kildare and is still celebrated on Saint Brigid's Day. On February 2, the Christian holiday of Candlemas, also known as the Festival of Lights, is celebrated to commemorate the purification of Saint Mary forty days after the birth of Jesus. Candlemas also welcomes the return of the light, much like the pagan Imbolc and Christian feast day of Saint Brigid. However, some maintain that Candlemas is actually derived from the ancient Roman holiday of Februalia, which honored Februus, the god of death and purification.

IMBOLC ALTAR

T he Imbolc altar brings a breath of fresh air into the home after the long months spent shuttered. Creating it on a table in the main room of the home will drive out stale energies while inviting new energies in.

MAGICKAL CORRESPONDENCES OF IMBOLC

ALTERNATIVE NAMES: Imbolg, Oimelc & Brigid's Day (Celtic), St. Brigid's Day and Candlemas (Christian), Februalia (Roman), Groundhog Day (North American)

COLORS: Green, red, white

CRYSTALS: Green aventurine, selenite, fluorite, clear quartz, rose quartz, citrine

DEITIES: Brigid, Ceres, and Vesta (Roman); Cerridwen (Celtic); Gaia, Hestia, and Pan (Greek); the Cailleach (Celtic)

ELEMENT: Earth/Air

FLOWERS, HERBS, AND TREES: Early bloomers (crocuses, daffodils, snowdrop, lily of the valley, iris), lemongrass, basil, chamomile, rosemary, melissa, clary sage, lavender, mint, frankincense, myrrh

FOODS: Milk, oats, seeds, honey, maple syrup, fruit, bannock bread, barmbrack

SYMBOLS: Brigid's cross, candle crown, hearth, cauldron, wells, wheels, fire

THEMES: Purification, blessing, healing, renewal, rebirth

Altar cloths in white and green, the traditional colors of Imbolc, signify the purification and growth associated with the season. A bed of grass or Irish moss can even serve as a living altar cloth or as base for green and white candles and crystals such as selenite and green aventurine. You may also dress the altar in green and white ribbons, fresh flowers, and herbs; early bloomers such as snowdrops, crocuses, and daffodils can bring vitality in pots or vases. An altar spray or incense made from herbaceous extracts of lemongrass, basil, chamomile, rosemary, melissa, or clary sage can freshen your sacred space and bring the scent of fertile ground into the home.

On this eve in old Ireland, tradition called for hearth fires in every home to be put out and then relit with the sacred flames of Brigid to welcome the Sun back to the land. Even if you do not have a fireplace in your home, incorporating candles, lanterns, a fireproof vessel, or twinkle lights in the southern direction of Fire on your altar can evoke the light and warmth of the Sun. If deities are in your practice, you might include a flower crown lit with candles, which is said to have been worn by the goddess Brigid.

To balance Brigid's eternal flame and the sun's triumphant return, water was often worshipped alongside fire at Imbolc. The Celts made pilgrimages to the sacred waters of Ireland's holy wells, which were thought to conceal entrances to the otherworld. At the well, it was customary for a young maiden to, upon drinking the water, ask the residing water spirit (often sprites or faeries) who she might marry. Once asleep beside the well, the maiden would promptly dream of her would-be suitor. Pilgrimages to soak in the restorative, healing powers of the spring-fed wells still occur today. To evoke the power of these sacred waters on your altar, include a small bowl or chalice of water from a natural source in the western direction of the element of Water. You may use this for anointing or sipping during divination or healing rituals. This water can also be used to set an intention or make a wish. In modern Ireland, it is still a tradition to ask for prosperity and blessings when visiting the wells. There, one might leave offerings of coins or clooties— small pieces of cloth that are dipped in the sacred water and tied to the tree branches above.

With the quickening of the earth comes the sowing of seeds. The Imbolc altar can act as a place to bless the seeds you will be planting in your fields or gardens, or as a sacred space to set your intentions—the metaphysical seeds that you will grow for the summer and fall harvests. You can include a small pad of parchment or birch paper and a pen at the altar for writing your intentions down. They can then be transformed into elemental energy by burning in the flame of the candles or in a fireproof vessel. Seeds are also represented in the foods of Imbolc. Small cakes and breads made from poppyseeds, sesame seeds, wheat, oat, dried fruits, and herbs are customary, and a small serving tray or cake plate could accompany your Imbolc altar. Bannock bread, an indigenous Scottish recipe, is a quick grain bread baked in a skillet. You may also choose to serve barmbrack, a traditional Irish soda bread.

As spring arrives, the pastures are being prepared for the birth of livestock. Imbolc's folk name of *Oimelc* translates to "milk of ewes" and signifies the start of lambing season. During this time of year, the ewes become full with milk as they nourish their babies in the lengthening sunlight. Flowing freely

The Imbolc altar can act as a place to bless the seeds you will be planting in your fields or gardens, or as a sacred space to set your intentions—the metaphysical seeds that you will grow for the summer and fall harvests.

across much of the ancient Celtic lands, this milk is used in a variety of ways, including bathing and baking. Foods made with milk and butter, particularly those infused with herbs, are often present at the Imbolc feast table; you might include herbed butter, sheep's cheese, or a butter cake. A small sipping bowl or chalice of fresh milk on the Imbolc altar in the western direction of the Water element honors the swelling of the season and the nourishment that is to come. Feel free to replace goat, cow, or plant-based milks with almond, soy, or coconut. Once you have consumed your fill of the milk, it is customary to leave the rest outside for the wildlife.

The Imbolc sky was closely monitored to predict when the ground could be broken for seed. If the weather was pleasant, it meant that the Cailleach, the Dark Mother said to be Brigid's counter goddess, who ruled the winter months, was out gathering wood for her fire because winter would not be retreating anytime soon. If the weather was rotten, it meant that the Cailleach had no need for collecting more firewood and had instead gone to bed; spring would soon arrive. The American holiday of Groundhog Day is reminiscent of such weather prediction.

If deities are in your practice, you might include a Brigid's cross constructed of rushes or reeds, or a Brideo'ga, a doll-like representation of Brigid. Herbs that are sacred to Brigid, such as sage, heather, violets, rosemary, and blackberry, can decorate the altar or be burned as incense.

SACRED HEARTH

Invite warmth and hope into the home.

Materials

Hearth (you may substitute a stand-alone wood stove or candelabra)

Pot or bowl of casting herbs such as calendula, sage, rosemary, lavender, basil, and chamomile

Pillar candles in warm colors

Gold candle holders or plates

Cauldron of naturally sourced water

Besom

Ash bucket

As the cold winter nights fell over ancient pagan lands, hearth fires warmed homes and comforted people. The fires cooked nourishing stews of bone and broth and filling, baked breads of oat and corn. They dried animal pelts and bundles of herbs while pottery was fired in the kiln. The light of the hearth fire was a place to escape the darkness that had settled over the fields, reigniting bonds strained by the Midwinter struggle. The roundhouses of the Iron Age accommodated the main hearth in the center of the dwelling, and, symbolically, there the hearth has remained—a central place of gathering at many homes.

Place a pot of purifying casting herbs at the base of the hearth. Casting these into the fire will clear the home of unwanted energies and release a fragrant scent to overcome the stale winter air. Place pillar candles in warm colors along the base of the hearth to symbolize the return of the Sun. You may insert them into gold candle holders or arrange them on golden plates representative of the Sun. As you light the candles from the main hearth fire, assign each an aspect of the Fire element (for example, ignites passion and creativity, encourages growth, stimulates life, purifies energy, and so on). If you have an open hearth or a rack above the fire, warm a cauldron of naturally sourced water to be saved as sacred water for your rituals. Place a besom—a broom used to symbolically sweep away negative energies—beside your hearth. By the besom, place a small bucket for collecting ash after Imbolc has ended and the fire has gone out. You can mix the ash with Dead Sea salt to make Witches' Black Salt, a potent protection salt for warding, or mix with water to make an ash paste for marking sigils. You may also spread the ashes over your fields or gardens or mix them with potting soil as fertilizer.

BRIGID'S SHRINE

Honor Brigid, the hearth goddess of Imbolc.

Materials

Metal tray

Jar candle with at least twenty-four hours of burn time

Cast-iron or forged bowl or skillet

Herbs and flowers of Brigid, such as heather, basil, blackberry, snowdrops, daffodils, coltsfoot, tansy, violets, and myrrh

Garnet or carnelian (optional)

Placard (optional)

Cauldron of well or spring water (In lieu of sacred water, you may cleanse and bless purified water with salt or light to fill your cauldron.)

Small jar of coins or brass rings

Woven basket

Edible offerings such as bread or seed cakes

Vase or copper jug of fragrant airy herbs or flowers such as lavender and mint

Representation of Brigid such as a Brigid statue, a Brideo'ga dolly (see page 47), Brigid's cross (see page 47), an altar card, or a flower crown of candles

Tools of Brigid, such as a blacksmith's hammer, a pen and paper for poetry or a lute for bards, and a mortar and pestle for healing

3 taper candles in white, green, and red

Chair and flowers and greenery with which to decorate it

According to Irish mythology, the hearth goddess Brigid descends from the legendary Tuatha Dé Danann— the supernatural race from which the fae folk and leprechauns of Irish folklore were born. Also known as the "Bright Arrow" or the "Bright One," Brigid was the keeper of the perpetual, sacred flame and was worshipped as a triple goddess who lit the fire under her aspects of healing, poetry, and smithcraft. In pagan times, her sacred flame was said to be tended for nineteen days at a time by nineteen maidens (after which it was tended by Brigid herself on the twentieth day) in her temple on the hill of Kildare. She was so beloved by her followers that even Christianization in the fifth century could not diminish her hold over the people of Ireland.

During the religious conversion, she was adopted as Saint Brigid, a patron Saint of Ireland, and her temple was converted to a monastery where her sacred flame lived on under the watch of nineteen Catholic nuns. Although the flame was extinguished and the holy well blocked during the sixteenth century's reformation, the Brigidine Sisters in Kildare reignited her flame in 1993, and it has burned ever since. Pilgrimages to Saint Brigid's Holy Well in Kildare still occur, and the evidence hangs upon the rag tree tied with clooties for good health and blessings. There, pilgrims are given stations at which to contemplate the different aspects of Brigid.

Because Brigid's sacred flame will be the central theme, forgoing the altar cloth in favor of a forged or hammered tray is not only practical but will bring Brigid's smith-craft aspect to the shrine. In the southern direction of the Fire element, place a jar candle in a cast-iron or forged bowl or skillet. Dress the area around the candle with herbs and flowers of Brigid. You may also include fiery crystals such as garnet and carnelian. If you like, make a placard or a label for the candle that says "Brigid's Sacred Flame." In the western direction of the Water element, place a cauldron of water sourced from a well or spring. Include a jar of coins or brass rings that can be tossed into the sacred water as offerings.

In some traditions, a tiny bed and a phallic-like wand known as a priapic wand that is made of a stick and acorn might accompany the dolly to invite the goddess to spend the night and bless you with fertility.

In the northern direction of the Earth element, place a woven basket of edible offerings such as buttered bread and seed cakes. In the eastern direction of the Air element, place a vase or copper jug of fragrant airy herbs or flowers such as lavender and mint. In the center of the shrine, place a Brigid statue, a Brideo'ga dolly, Brigid's cross, an altar card, or a flower crown of candles. A Brideo'ga corn dolly can be made from the husks of corn and dressed in red, white, and green. In some traditions, a tiny bed and a phallic-like wand known as a priapic wand that is made of a stick and acorn might accompany the dolly to invite the goddess to spend the night and bless you with fertility.

To make Brigid's cross, weave reeds or wheat rushes into the shape of a four-armed cross with a square in the middle. This shape symbolizes the Sun, which brings fertility, prosperity, and health to the home. Include some of Brigid's tools of the trade in the remaining space on the shrine. Around the central sacred flame, place three taper candles in white, green, and red, one for each of her aspects. Be sure to light these and any other Imbolc candles from the sacred flame in your jar candle. Place a chair in front of the shrine and dress it with flowers and greenery so that you may sit and contemplate how you might invite Brigid's aspects into your own practice.

ENTRYWAY CLEANSING SPACE

Cleanse your home of stagnant, winter energies.

Materials

Green or white altar cloth

Small table or stand for altar

Bucket and cheesecloth

Botanical floor wash (see below)

Imbolc anointing oil (see below)

Small fireproof vessel or incense burner

Frankincense and myrrh incense

Pale yellow candle

Selenite or clear quartz crystal wand

**Herbal bundle for smoke cleansing
or lavender**

Small bowl of salt

Besom

Amongst the pagan homes of yesteryear, the end of winter meant that the stale energy of hibernation could finally be exorcised. As Imbolc arrived, the windows and doors were flung open and homes were cleansed of dust and debris. Ill-intentioned spirits that had sought safe harbor in dark, pest-ridden corners were swept out, and the cloak of darkness that weighed heavily on the body and soul was lifted. Walls and floors were scrubbed from top to bottom and first flowers brought in as the home was transformed into a garden of possibility.

Transforming your spring-cleaning routine into one of intention can ensure that you are not only physically cleansing your space, but clearing the energetic footprint left behind by winter. In the entryway of your home, place a large white or green altar cloth on a small table or stand. Make a botanical floor wash by steeping a handful of dried lavender and sage in hot water for ten minutes and then straining through cheesecloth into a bucket. Add a few fresh orange or lemon slices, a cup of vinegar, and a few drops each of lavender and lemongrass essential oils. This can be used to cleanse your floors. In a small dropper bottle, create an Imbolc anointing oil made from jojoba or olive oil and a few drops each of lemongrass and lavender essential oils with which to dust your wooden furniture. In the southern direction of the Fire element, place a small fireproof vessel to burn frankincense and myrrh incense. To draw the element of Air to the altar, place a pale yellow candle in the East. Here, you may also want to include a wand made of selenite or clear quartz for the vibrational cleansing of each room. An herbal smoke bundle such as sage or lavender or an herbal spray can also be used to botanically cleanse the air. In the northern direction of the Earth element, place a small bowl of salt for sprinkling across thresholds. Above the altar, hang a besom for ritual sweeping of negative and unwanted energies.

RITUAL BATH ALTAR TRAY

Cleanse and replenish your spirit.

Materials

Bathtub, washtub, or foot soak tub

Small white altar cloth

Wooden bath caddy or tray

White or ivory votive candles or tealights

Bath tea: Imbolc herbs such as angelica, lavender, and lemon balm placed in a small muslin bag

Imbolc anointing oil (see page 49)

Small pitcher of warm, sweet milk mixed with honey

Small bowl

Cleansing, healing, light-drawing, and nurturing crystals such as rose quartz, clear quartz, and amethyst

Soft white face cloth

Lavender essential oil

Although the physical space that you occupy has now been cleared of negative energy, the metaphysical space in which your spirit dwells must also be cleansed. At Imbolc, you might find it necessary to shed the unhealthy or toxic habits that have accumulated during the winter months. This is the time of purification—of clearing old ways to make room for new growth. One of the easiest (and most relaxing) ways to accomplish this is through ritual bathing. The concept of cleansing the body and spirit before performing purposeful work is common across many cultures and religions. Not only does it ensure we are keeping our vessels free from actual dirt and germs that could spread beyond our control, but it prepares our spiritual fields for planting.

This ritual should be performed in a private space, either in a bathroom or a washtub set in the garden. If you do not have a bathtub, a foot soak tub will do. Place a small white altar cloth in a wooden bath caddy or tray. Arrange white or ivory votive or tea candles on the tray. Steep your cleansing bath tea in the warm water. On the tray, include the bottle of Imbolc anointing oil you made for the entryway cleansing space, and place a few drops in the bath to nurture your skin and spirit. If deities are in your practice, a small pitcher of warm sweet milk mixed with honey can call forth the blessings of Brigid. In a small bowl, gather cleansing, healing, and light-drawing crystals such as rose quartz, clear quartz, and amethyst so that they may be placed in the water or along the rim of the bathtub. Include a soft white face cloth that has been anointed with just one or two drops of lavender essential oil for placing over your eyes and soothing your mind and spirit.

SEED BLESSING SHRINE

Create a space for your intentions to take root.

Materials

Garden bench or shelf

Green altar cloth

Bowl of soil

Baskets of seeds and bulbs

Priapic wand

Crystals for growth: green aventurine, moss agate, malachite, clear quartz, and citrine

Gardening tools such as spades, garden gloves, and bulb diggers (optional)

Bell or singing bowl

Statue of Brigid or other fertility deity (optional)

The festival of Imbolc stirs the beginnings of new life. The snow is melting, and spring's first flowers are beginning to poke through the softening soil. At this time, seeds are not only physically planted but spiritually planted so that intentions may take root. The blessing of seeds harks back to ancient agricultural times when gods and goddesses reigned over the crop fields and offerings were made to ensure a successful growing season. Brigid, Ceres (the Roman goddess of agriculture), and Gaia (the Greek earth mother), amongst other agricultural or fertility gods and goddesses, were prayed to as the seeds were consecrated. Even if deities are not in your practice, nurturing, honoring, and charging your seeds with your energy can encourage a bountiful harvest.

In your garden shed or on your patio, set up a garden bench or shelf for your seed shrine in the eastern direction of the sunrise. Place a green altar cloth down on the surface to symbolize growth and catch any wayward soil or water. Place a bowl of soil in the center so that you may ceremoniously plant a seed or bulb that you gathered at Mabon. Around this bowl, place baskets containing the packets of your seeds or bags of bulbs. You may also include a fertility-ensuring priapic wand for ritually blessing the seeds. Around the shrine, create a crystal growth grid with green aventurine, moss agate, malachite, clear quartz, and citrine. Include gardening tools like spades, garden gloves, and bulb diggers as well as a bell or singing bowl for vibrational tuning. If deities are in your practice, place a statue of Brigid or another fertility god or goddess on the shrine to call forth their blessings. Allow this shrine to stand until planting time, so that you may greet the seeds each morning, playing music or ringing the bell or bowl to energize them and attune them with the frequency of nature.

INTENTION CIRCLE

Set your intentions in preparation for the growing season.

Materials

Herbed salt: coarse sea salt and herbs of Imbolc such as lavender, lemon balm, rosemary, sage, angelica, basil, and bay

4 elemental candles (red: Fire; yellow: Air; blue: Water; green: Earth)

Cast-iron pot

Small plate or bowl of bay leaves

Pen or marker

When you set intentions, you are planting the seeds that will blossom into your future. In the altars and rituals prior to this one, we have cleared the way for new growth, fertilized the fields, and blessed the seeds, and now we must plant. But planting does not begin and end at sticking the seed in the soil. For a fruitful bounty, great care must be taken throughout the entire process. Temperature, sunlight, water, soil quality, and location must all be considered. Depth of planting, too, is crucial to the seeds' survival. Too deep and sunlight will not reach them; too shallow and the soil will not shelter them. There are wild creatures, too, who scavenge the fields looking for a meal, and they will come at every stage of growth. Like a farmer who has cultivated the wilderness, you must learn to protect your crops. This is a metaphor for your ideas, your goals, and your happiness. Consider all possibilities and evaluate your path from every angle. Protect and nurture your intentions and they will be big and strong come harvest.

An intention circle is a sacred and safe place for you to plant your seeds, and it is best if you use your working altar. Cast a small circle with herbed salt crafted from coarse sea salt and herbs of Imbolc such as lavender, lemon balm, rosemary, sage, angelica, basil, and bay—sprinkling it in a clockwise direction. Call the energies of the elements to your altar by placing candles of each elemental color in their cardinal directions. Place a cast-iron pot in the center of the circle. Next to the pot, place a small plate or bowl of bay leaves and a pen or marker. Here, you may write your intentions on the bay leaves and burn them in the pot. Once the leaves have reduced to ash, scatter the ash across a field, garden, or orchard or mix it into your potting soil so that your intentions will grow right along with the plants.

CHAPTER 3

SPRING EQUINOX

Northern Hemisphere: March 21; Southern Hemisphere: September 21

In perfect balance, light and dark hang above the budding land as the Vernal Equinox ushers in the official start of spring. On its way to its highest position in our sky, the Sun journeys across the celestial equator—the sphere of stars and heavenly bodies whose midline intersects with the terrestrial equator. It is during this time of the year that day and night are of equal length. For approximately twelve hours, your region of the Earth will face the Sun squarely, receiving all its splendor and warmth, until it turns away for the night and immerses itself in its own shadow.

In astrology, the Spring Equinox marks the beginning of the year and the season of Aries. However, on the Wheel of the Year, it is considered the midway point between the solstices at Midwinter and Midsummer. No matter the timing, the equinox brings with it the gentle breeze and budding plants of the first official day of spring for many of the northern regions. Mayans referred to this time as the "return of the sun serpent," because the Sun appeared to slither down the steps of the pyramid at Chichen Itza. Germanic tribes celebrated Ostara and the lunar goddess and spring maiden, Ēostre. When the Romans invaded the Germanic regions, a Christianized version of Ostara emerged—Easter. Modern pagan celebrations center around the ancient traditions associated with Ostara and celebrate the Sun on its journey toward greater illumination. Although there is no clear sightline of the rising equinox Sun through the stones of Stonehenge, it is a popular place for neo-Druids and pagans alike to celebrate the equinox as the Sun rises over the stones. There, they welcome the growth of the season, knowing that darkness is a necessary adversary of light. The equinox helps us to find balance between the illuminated self and the shadow self, and it is the opportune time to seek out the hidden self so that we may forge a new path through the darkness.

OSTARA ALTAR

O stara's altar is teeming with renewal. Life has emerged once again from the frozen ground and signs of spring are everywhere. If it is warm and blooming where you live, you may want to create your Ostara altar outdoors in the garden or on the patio so that it receives a breath of fresh air.

MAGICKAL CORRESPONDENCES OF OSTARA

ALTERNATIVE NAMES: Vernal Equinox, Spring Equinox, Ēostre and Ēostre's Day (Germanic), Easter (Christian), Alban Eilir (Druidic), Bacchanalia (Roman)

COLORS: Pastels, yellow, green, lilac, pink, baby blue

CRYSTALS: Amethyst, rose quartz, moonstone, aquamarine

DEITIES: Ēostre (Germanic), Gaia (Greek), Venus (Roman), Isis (Egyptian), Adonis (Greek), Odin (Norse)

ELEMENT: Air

FLOWERS, HERBS, AND TREES: Daffodils, tulips, irises, lilies, violets, hyacinth, lily of the valley, lilac, jasmine, meadowsweet, borage, mint, basil, lemon balm, tansy, thyme, willow, hawthorne, dogwood

FOODS: Egg dishes, sweets, spring salads, fish, hot cross buns, ham, lamb, milk, honey

SYMBOLS: Ēostre, eggs, rabbits, hares, robins, lambs, butterflies, bees, faeries, seeds, soil

THEMES: New life, fertility, rebirth, renewal, growth, balance, harmony, health

If the altar is indoors, put it in a light-filled space with a view of the outside. The altar should face the East—the direction of the rising Sun as well as of the spring season and the element of Air. An altar cloth of lilac, rose, yellow, or green or one of moss or grass can be placed on the surface and decorated with candles of light pink, blue, yellow, or lilac and crystals of nurturing and growth such as rose quartz, amethyst, and green aventurine.

Fertility, a symbol of the season, is not just for the birds and bees, but also for your mind and spirit. Incorporating eggs, hares, and seeds into your Ostara altar can encourage growth of ideas and creativity. Fragrant wildflowers and herbs, too, can bring fresh color to your space while physically and symbolically cleaning the air. Violets, daffodils, lilies, tulips, hyacinths, lilac, lily of the valley, and irises as well as herbs such as mint, basil, borage, and lemon balm can all be planted quite early in the season, even outdoors, and enjoyed by Ostara in many northern regions. On your main Ostara altar, you can keep cut flowers in vases or potted plants in earthenware pots. You may also include floral or herbal incense or sprays of jasmine, sage, apple blossom, or lavender.

The first day of spring is also the perfect time to focus on any prosperity rituals you may have been planning. If you like, include a honey jar on your Ostara altar. Honey jars are thought to have been introduced to modern paganism by Hoodoo practitioners from the southern United States. They work on many levels to sweeten both romantic and business relationships. Start with a four-ounce glass jar and fill it with honey that has been infused with herbs associated with wealth, opportunity, or luck, such as chamomile, patchouli, alfalfa, mint, basil, bay, or thyme. Include a coin, dollar bill, or gold pieces in the jar and close the lid. On top of the lid, dress a green votive candle with a prosperity oil made from chamomile and mint-infused olive oil. If your honey jar is properly tended

Fertility, a symbol of the season, is not just for the birds and bees, but also for your mind and spirit. Incorporating eggs, hares, and seeds into your Ostara altar can encourage growth of ideas and creativity.

with intention and magick, you can expect to receive an increase in wealth once the candle has burned down.

The Ostara feast draws from the growth of the season: fresh salads, lamb, ambrosia, deviled eggs, and hot cross buns—pastries with crosses pressed into the tops—can be displayed on your main altar or alongside it on the feast table. Although crosses are typically associated with the Christian season of Lent, they have also come to symbol-ize pagan themes that come in groups of four, such as the elements or the cardinal directions. Ham, lamb, and fish are also typically consumed at this time as the fields and rivers teem with new life. They are often prepared with spring herbs as well as the milk and butter of Imbolc traditions. Edible delights, however, are not the only thing nature is busy creating during the season of Ostara; medicinal herbs, too, begin to fill the meadows and woodlines. On a small tray, include any medicinal teas or tonics that you have crafted from blood-cleansing, early spring greens such as dandelion and burdock.

Although Ostara typically calls for one of the more colorful altars on the Wheel of the Year, the arrival of the equinox would not be replete without the black

Although crosses are typically associated with the Christian season of Lent, they have also come to symbolize pagan themes that come in groups of four, such as the elements or the cardinal directions.

and white representation of the two halves of the year. At the equinox, light and dark are in balance, each exerting an equal force on your magick. Honor this balance with black and white candles, symbols such as the yin and yang, or a Sun and Moon. This visual representation of light and dark can help you focus on your shadow self—the inner you that contains your deepest, darkest truths. How can you acknowledge it and grow from it?

If deities are in your practice, you may want to include a statue of Ēostre, the Germanic dawn goddess and spring maiden for which Ostara is named. In some duotheistic neo-pagan traditions such as Wicca, the Horned God—the masculine divinity associated with nature—is also called upon during Ostara. His young form, sometimes associated with the god Pan, welcomes the budding of spring with the goddess as they dance and hunt their way across the land.

REAWAKENING MEDITATION CIRCLE

Awaken and energize your magick.

Materials

**Colorful spring flowers and herbs
such as chamomile, sage, daffodils,
lilies, and hyacinths**

**Cleansing and charging crystals
such as selenite, clear quartz,
amethyst, blue kyanite, and citrine**

**4 elemental pillar candles
(red: Fire; yellow: Air;
blue: Water; green: Earth)**

**Loose incense such as sage, lavender,
cedar, frankincense, and myrrh**

Fireproof pot

Feather or fan

Bell or singing bowl

Across the land, sleepy buds poke through
the ground, stretching their green leaves out
to greet the Sun. After months of slumbering
under a thick winter blanket, life is emerging
and awakening. And just like nature, our
spirit and magick must be reawakened.
During the winter, we slowed our momen
tum. We tended to our hearth and home
and reflected on all that dwelled inside.
Now, it is time to let it go and begin anew.
Reawakening your magick is like cleansing and charging a crystal. When negative
energies accumulate, our vibrational output

changes. Our auras shrink and our magick
dims. Reawakening our magick is a way to
bring it back to its optimum output, its true
frequency. This meditation circle is perfect for
beginning new projects, letting go of what
no longer serves you, and making space for
new growth.

Find a quiet spot outdoors, such as in a forest
glade, a secluded garden, or the edge of or
dock on a calm water body. If the outdoors is
not accessible, choose a private space where
you can open the windows and feel the fresh
air circulate. In a circle large enough for
you to sit or stand inside, arrange colorful
herbs and flowers such as chamomile, sage,
daffodils, lilies, and hyacinths and cleansing/
charging stones such as selenite, clear quartz,
amethyst, blue kyanite, and citrine. At each
quarter, place a pillar candle in the corresponding color to the elements (red: South;
yellow: East; blue: West; green: North) with
the symbols of the elements carved into the
candles with a carving knife. Burn loose
incense in a fireproof pot in the middle of
the circle. Place a feather or fan and a bell
or singing bowl next to it. After calling the
elements, face East and begin to cleanse and
charge your magick by wafting the herbal
smoke with a feather or fan over your body.
Ring the bell or bowl and allow it to attune
your magick with the frequency of nature.

BALANCE CIRCLES

Illuminate and integrate your shadow self.

Materials

Table or desk

Tumbled black (black tourmaline, onyx, obsidian, or hematite), white or clear (selenite, quartz, moonstone, or calcite), and gray (gray agate, smoky quartz, lodestone, or labradorite) crystals

Black altar cloth (optional)

Tealight

Anointing oil infused with plant allies for shadow work such as rosemary (protection), lavender (calming), and mugwort (introspection)

When we think of light and dark, we must realize that they are rooted in dependence— you cannot have one without the other. This is balance. There can be no illumination without shadow and no shadow without illumination. The shadow self, the dark part of us that resides deep within, is constructed of elements that we often acknowledge as "bad." We suppress these elements, burying them so deeply in our subconscious that they never see the light of day. But there, they fester in the inescapable darkness, weighing us down and hindering our capability for growth. By illuminating and transforming these elements, we can integrate them to achieve a balance of the whole self.

For this altar, choose a private, indoor space such as a bedroom or an attic nook. On a table or desk, create a two-circle Venn diagram—an *intersection*—with crystals. If you like, you may use a black altar cloth on which you have drawn the circles in paint or chalk as a template. The stone circle on the left should be made with black crystals to represent the shadow self, while the circle on the right should be made of white or clear crystals for the illuminated self. The section where the two circles meet should be created out of gray crystals. In the dark circle, light a tealight anointed with an oil. As you meditate on this light, allow it to illuminate your shadow self. Gaze at the thoughts, feelings, and habits that reside there, and think about how you might integrate them into your illuminated self. How can each shadow be brought into a safe, constructive space? As you fulfill each meditation, remove a black stone from the shadow circle and place a gray stone in the intersecting space between the two circles to represent the shadow's integration.

DECORATED EGG BASKET

Provide a protected place for your intentions to grow.

Materials

Boiled eggs (Note: In lieu of poultry eggs, you can paint wooden or plaster eggs or display golden, chocolate, porcelain, Faberge, or pysanky eggs.)

Wax crayon

Plant-based dyes: vinegar and water infused with fresh materials such as beets, spinach, red cabbage, coffee, paprika, grape skins, and onion skins

Paper and pen

Wax seal

Woven basket of willow or oak

Moss or grass

Dried spring herbs such as lavender, mint, lemon balm, and sage

In the nooks and crannies of barns and sheds, in the hollows of trees and bluebird houses, and even cradled in the tangled thickets of thorny bushes lie nests of eggs laid in the awakening of spring. Since ancient times, eggs have been associated with the concepts of rebirth, renewal, and fertility. In German folklore, the goddess Ēostre was said to take pity on an injured bird, transforming him into a hare and bestowing on him the ability to lay colorful eggs. He was so unexpectedly prolific in his egg-laying, however, that she became jealous of his affairs and cast him into the sky as the constellation Lepus under the Hunter, Orion. Each spring, she allowed him to come down from the sky and gift colorful eggs to all the children.

On the morning of Ostara, prepare boiled eggs. Once they're cool, draw symbols of intention for love, fertility, or growth such as hearts, circles, or ankhs in wax on them. Color them with plant-based dyes by soaking them in natural blends of vinegar and plant-infused water made with fresh materials such as beets, spinach, red cabbage, coffee, paprika, grape skins, and onion skins. In lieu of wax writing, you may write your intentions on pieces of paper and wrap them around the eggs, sealing each with a wax seal. In a woven basket of willow or oak, create a bed of moss or grass as well as dried spring herbs to cradle the eggs. This basket will be a symbol of the nest from which new life springs forth, and it will protect your intentions as they grow. After you have completed your growth or fertility rituals with the eggs, you can either eat them to grow your intentions from within, or bury them in the garden so that your intentions grow with the plants.

HERB SHELF

Encourage the growth of your intentions.

Materials

Green altar cloth

Natural pots such as terra cotta, earthenware, ceramic, or peat

Potting soil

Seeds that you blessed during Imbolc or seedlings

Small watering can

Green aventurine crystal

Bell or small singing bowl

Fireproof pot or incense burner

Intention paper and pen

The herbs of the Spring Equinox are sacred for the magickal workings of fertility and growth spells. Early herbs such as dandelion, lamb's quarters, chickweed, nettle, elderflower, lemon balm, mint, borage, basil, chamomile, sage, and violet all burst forth from the soil before the hot summer Sun takes hold of the land. Along with their wide-ranging medicinal usage and the nutrients they bring to salads, soups, teas, and smoothies, these herbs can add their vibratory energy to any spells centered on increase. This is particularly true when you nurture them from seed—the very beginning of life. Growing them in a sacred, magickal space will endear them to your vibratory makeup as you work in symbiosis.

Create your sacred herb shelf on an eastern-facing sunny shelf or windowsill, and lay down a green altar cloth to represent the growth of the season. Fill pots until they are three-quarters full of potting soil. In each pot, plant the seeds that you blessed during Imbolc. Because this will be a living and breathing altar, you will want to call upon the elements of nature. In the West, place a small watering can; in the North, a green aventurine stone; in the East, a bell or small singing bowl to tap into the vibratory energy of the budding seeds; and in the South, a small fireproof pot or incense burner to keep pests and negative energy at bay. On small pieces of paper, write your intentions for the year ahead, and place them under each of the pots so that you may watch them grow with the plants. Once the seedlings have two sets of leaves, you may continue to grow them on your herb shelf or transfer them to larger pots or a garden space. Now, you have your very own magickally tended herbs to dry, infuse, and use in magickal workings for growth, new beginnings, love, and fertility spells.

GROWTH GROTTO

Create a nurturing space for your ideas and talents.

Materials

Stones, branches, or vines such as climbing roses, wisteria, and ivy, and an arbor

Green linens or silks

Natural or artificial foliage

Growth crystals such as green aventurine, green calcite, moss agate, tree agate, and rhyolite

Colorful spring flowers such as violets, daffodils, crocuses, irises, and hyacinths

Green altar cloth

Stone or glass bowl

Pitcher

Naturally sourced water

Growth herbs such as alfalfa, mint, thyme, chamomile, patchouli, and basil

With the arrival of spring comes boundless energy for growth. Across the land, new life is sprouting at a rapid rate as the world around us blossoms in the expanding light. Ostara is the perfect time of the year to focus on growing your creativity, expanding your knowledge, increasing your wealth, or even creating new life. This type of work is best performed in a sacred space surrounded by lush growth—evidence of the energy that abounds. A grotto is a small cave, either naturally occurring or manmade, that offers its cavernous silence to those seeking a private retreat for devotional worship. In antiquity, grottoes were a popular feature of Greek and Roman architecture and often housed mythological and sacred waters. Today, artificial grottoes can be used in much the same way.

For this sacred space, construct a small grotto by building one out of stones or branches, or hang vines such as climbing roses, wisteria, and ivy over an arbor. If you do not have an outdoor space available to you, you can use the space under a desk or table; drape curtains or hanging plants over the "entrance" to give it a garden-like feel. Decorate the outside of the grotto in green linens or silks, natural or artificial foliage, and growth crystals like green aventurine, green calcite, moss agate, tree agate, and rhyolite. If you like, add colorful spring flowers to the foliage. Inside, lay a green altar cloth on a flat surface and place a stone or glass bowl on the cloth. Fill a pitcher with naturally sourced water and solar infuse it with growth-encouraging herbs such as alfalfa, mint, thyme, chamomile, patchouli, and basil by placing it out in the rising Sun. Pour this sacred water into the bowl and anoint your solar plexus chakra (the growth center of the body) and pulse points as they circulate your life force. You may also use the water to consecrate your magickal tools.

CHAPTER 4

BELTANE

Northern Hemisphere: May 1; Southern Hemisphere: November 1

Beltane is the cross-quarter holiday between the Spring Equinox and the Summer Solstice and the second of four Celtic fire festivals in the Wheel of the Year. In Gaelic, the word *Beltane* means "lucky fire," a fitting description for the celebration of the coronation feast of the Celtic Sun god Belenus. At sunrise on Beltane, the Bronze Age Beltany Stone Circle in the northwest of Ireland displays an incredible view of the Sun as it emerges from the top of the only decorated stone in the circle. It is thought that this is representative of the great bonfires that were lit atop the village hill in ancient pagan times.

Other cultures, too, have celebrated the transition to summer in May. The Christians of Germany, for example, celebrated Walpurgis Night in honor of Saint Walpurga's canonization. The ancient Romans honored Flora, the goddess of flowers, with the festival of Floralia.

On the old Irish calendar, Beltane marks the beginning of summer as it stands on the precipice between the two halves of the year, leading us from dark to light and from growth to harvest. It is considered a liminal time in which the veil between the human and supernatural world is thin. Witches, faeries, and other nature spirits are free to roam—thus, many ancient pagans took protective measures against meddlesome enchantments. Along with Samhain, it is considered one of the most powerful times of the year for spirit communication and divination rituals. Modern Beltane celebrations combine many of the ancient pagan traditions, but they often focus on the abundance and passion that the transition between spring and summer brings. Love, sex, fertility, and marriage or handfastings are common themes of the Beltane festival and are represented by the union of the god and goddess.

BELTANE ALTAR

T he Beltane altar is as colorful and lively as the flowers that blanket the late spring meadows. Decorating it with vibrant blooms, lush greenery, symbols of fertility, and the virile flames of the Bel Fire can bring beauty and vitality into your sacred space.

MAGICKAL CORRESPONDENCES OF BELTANE

ALTERNATIVE NAMES: Walpurgis Night (Germanic), May Day (Anglo-Saxon), Floralia (Roman)

COLORS: Green, violet, yellow, pink, sky blue, rose red

CRYSTALS: Rose quartz, green aventurine, fluorite, emerald, tourmaline, rainbow moonstone, bloodstone

DEITIES: Walpurgis (Christian), Freya (Norse), the May Queen (Anglo-Saxon), Flora (Roman), Gaia (Greek), Creiddylad (Welsh)

ELEMENT: Air/Fire

FLOWERS, HERBS, AND TREES: Hawthorn, rowan, lily of the valley, cowslip, peony, rose, lilac, cornflower, lavender, foxgloves, heather, honeysuckles, forsythia, dandelion, rosemary, lemon balm, mint, mugwort, woodruff, and coltsfoot.

FOODS: Mead, honey, oats, breads and cakes, early summer vegetables, salads

SYMBOLS: Fire, flower crown or garland, May basket, maypole, May bough or bush, flowers, ribbons, hawthorn

THEMES: Rebirth, purification, blessing, beauty, spirit communication, protection, fertility/pregnancy, marriage, abundance

At the base of the Beltane altar should be an altar cloth in the emerald green of the lush, summer grass. Decorate it with a garland of early summer flowers such as roses, geraniums, pansies, peonies, daisies, and primroses as well as pillar or taper candles in the colors of the rainbow. You may also include crystals that vibrate positive and fertile energy, such as rose quartz, bloodstone, emerald, and green aventurine.

As a fire festival, Beltane celebrates all that the element contributes to life here on Earth: passion, stimulation, purification, and protection. In ancient times on the eve of Beltane, two hilltop bonfires raged until dawn as a symbol of the return of the Sun. It doubled as a purification and fertility rite. Cattle were driven between the fires on their way out to pasture to cleanse them of disease and bless them with fertility. The sacred fire of Beltane was also an invocation to the Celtic Sun god, Belenus, and was often referred to as the "Bel Fire." Dancing, handfasting, and cleansing rituals were performed around the fires. The home, too, was graced by the fires of Beltane—villagers would often put out their hearth fires and relight them with candles or torches ignited by the Beltane fire to bring its blessings into the home.

Once the fires were out, their ashes were spread over the fields to ensure a productive harvest. Including fire on your Beltane altar can bring good luck, prosperity, love, cleansing, protection, and eternal bonding to your home. You may want to have a small fireproof pot in which you burn herbs and charcoal or incense of the season, such as jasmine, sage, tuberose, passionflower, vanilla, sandalwood, mugwort, rosemary, lemon balm, mint, lavender, woodruff, and rose. Or you could use a jar candle or lantern surrounded by a base of oak or birch twigs to symbolize the bel fire.

Flowers are another important symbol of Beltane. They represent the abundance that the season brings. The beauty of colorful blooms graces the land on this turn of the wheel, and they are often used in flower crowns, garlands, and wreaths. The circular shape symbolizes the cycle of life and the rebirth of the Sun. The ancient pagans often wore garlands on their heads in celebration or tossed them into streams or ponds as an offering to the water spirits. You can create your own flower crown to include on your Beltane altar by shaping twigs of willow or apple branches and weaving flowers along the circle. Another popular way to celebrate the flowers of Beltane was to decorate the "May bush."

The May bush was often a hawthorn tree in a farmyard or village center that was decorated with yellow flowers such as primrose, witch hazel, and rowan as well as colorful ribbons and candles. "May baskets" full of flowers and sweets might be gifted to a friend or neighbor as a blessing or hung on the door of a hopeful lad's sweetheart. If you like, include a May basket on your altar to gift to a friend or lover.

The beauty of May Day is not only reserved for the flowers, however. The morning dew of Beltane was thought to have magickal powers, and young maidens often collected it from the hawthorn trees in hopes that washing their face with it would preserve their youthful beauty. If you like, include a small bottle of this sacred water on your main altar to anoint yourself or consecrate your tools.

Fertility and commitment rites such as maypole dancing, fire jumping, courtship rituals, and handfasting were performed in celebration of the abundance of the season to symbolically awaken the fertility of the land. The maypole, once a living tree dressed with flowers and greenery, was cut down, trimmed, and erected in the center of old English villages. It was woven, during a dance,

The morning dew of Beltane was thought to have magickal powers, and young maidens often collected it from the hawthorn trees in hopes that washing their face with it would preserve their youthful beauty.

with colorful ribbons to represent the intertwining of the male and female energies. This weaving of the ribbons —the symbolic union of the May Queen and King (or the God and Goddess in Wicca)— represents a love that has matured from the playful jaunts of Imbolc and will soon birth the harvest.

If deities are in your practice, you may want to hold a wedding feast for the Goddess and the Green Man to celebrate their union. At this time, the Goddess takes on the Horned God as her lover and becomes pregnant. Scottish oat cakes, early summer fruits and vegetables, and breads are all traditional early summer foods that can be represented on their wedding feast table. You may also want to include a

traditional May bowl—a bowl filled with wine or punch in which spring flowers such as woodruff are soaked (be careful not to use poisonous flowers such as daffodils and lily of the valley, amongst others). Beltane is also when the May Queen reigns supreme over the dark mother, the Cailleach, so you may want to celebrate her enthroning by including a statue of Flora (Roman), Creiddylad (Welsh), Gaia (Greek), Freya (Norse), or other fertility or mother goddess that has been dressed in white garb and flowers. Nature spirits, too, are quite active during Beltane, and it is thought that if you want to view the faeries, you simply need to twist a rowan branch into a circle and peer through it.

FIRE PIT OF PROTECTION

Cleanse and protect your body and spirit.

Materials

Stones, portable fire pit, or cast-iron pot

Kindling and logs

Wine, mead, or salt

Beltane greenery and flowers

Purification and protection crystals such as clear quartz, amethyst, and black tourmaline

Purifying and protective herbs or resins such as sage, lavender, cedar, thyme, frankincense, and myrrh

Jar or tin

The fires of Beltane not only represent the return of the Sun but act as a ritual cleansing of the land. In ancient farming practices, the smoke from the fires was used to drive pests and evil spirits away from the fields and cleanse the livestock of disease on their way out to pasture. Around the hilltop bel fire, villagers danced and jumped over the flames as a rite of purification for their body and spirit. Burning embers or torches lit from the fire would be taken back to the village homes to reignite their hearth fires with the sacred, protective flames. The ashes from the Beltane bonfires were kept as protective amulets in homes and spread over crops.

Construct your fire pit out of stone, a portable fire pit, or a cast-iron pot. Gather kindling and logs from any or all of the sacred trees of the Druids, and bless the wood by sprinkling wine, mead, or salt on the logs. Decorate the outside of the fire pit with Beltane greenery and flowers as well as crystals of purification and protection. Once the fire has been lit, cast purifying and protective herbs into the flames. You can then perform any of the rituals of the ancients: dance around or meditate on the flames and ask them for protection throughout the growing season; pass your magickal tools through the smoke to cleanse them; light your hearth fire and any candles you might have in your home or on your altars from the bel fire; and after the fire has gone out, sow the ash into soil or save some in a jar or tin for use in warding rituals or spells.

Note: *If you do not have access to an outdoor space, represent the bel fire with a jar candle. Decorate the base of the candle with stones and bark from the sacred trees.*

BEAUTY VANITY

Beckon health, luck, and beauty—both inside and out.

Materials

Clean, natural-fiber cloth

Jar

Cheesecloth

Decorative glass pitcher

Pink altar cloth or silver tray

Beltane flowers such as hawthorne, peonies, roses, lilies, irises, geranium, and lavender

Crystal facial roller or healing crystals such as rose quartz, amethyst, aquamarine, blue lace agate, jade, and lepidolite

Pink and white pillar or taper candles or a pink Himalayan salt candle holder

Glass bowl

Beltane is one of the traditional "well-dressing" holidays during which it was time to visit sacred wells in search of fertility, love, health, and beauty. The morning dew, too, was considered by many a maiden to be good luck to gather come Beltane. Washing one's face in dew gathered from the hawthorn tree at the break of May was thought to bring eternal health, luck, and beauty to the beholder. An old English nursery rhyme tells of the fair maid who enchants herself with the dew of the hawthorn tree:

The fair maid who, the first of May,
Goes to the fields at the break of day,
And washes in dew from the
hawthorn tree,
Will ever after handsome be.

At sunrise on Beltane, run a natural-fiber cloth across an open field of grass until it is heavy with moisture. Wring the cloth out into a glass jar and repeat until the jar is full. Filter the dew through cheesecloth, and collect it into a decorative glass pitcher. Place the pitcher on a pink altar cloth or silver tray on your vanity or bathroom counter. Decorate it with Beltane flowers and a crystal facial roller or healing crystals. Add pink and white pillar or taper candles or a pink Himalayan salt candle holder. Pour the dew water from the pitcher into a bowl, and gently splash it on your face for radiance inside and out. This holy dew water of May can also be used in glamour, love, and beauty spells. If deities are in your practice, Beltane dew is thought to be sacred to the ancient Roman goddess Diana, also known as "The Dewy One."

Note: *If you are not able to collect dew, source spring water and charge it with the rising Beltane Sun.*

FERTILITY GARLAND

Create a nurturing space to perform increase spells and fertility work.

Materials

Crystals of increase and fertility such as citrine, green aventurine, moonstone, jade, and carnelian

Herbs of increase and fertility, such as rosemary, myrtle, and basil

Seeds and fruits such as pomegranates, apples, and figs

Beltane flowers such as roses, poppies, jasmine, orchids, lilies, and lotuses

Greenery such as moss, ferns, rowan, oak, and hawthorne

Apple blossom incense

Feather or fan

Anointing oil: blend of evening primrose, pomegranate, and sweet orange oils

Compostable bag or box

During Beltane, the fertility energies of the blossoming land reach their height. It is the most powerful time of the year for growth spells, whether they be to conceive a child, generate new ideas, or bring fruition to business opportunities. In ancient pagan times, couples harnessed the fertile energy of May Eve by going "a-Maying"—making love in the fields and woods throughout the night

in hopes that they might conceive a child. The next morning, they would emerge with flowers and blossoming hawthorne branches to bless their barns and homes. The Beltane flowers were made into crowns or garlands to evoke their powers of attraction in the shape of the cycle of life.

On the eve of Beltane, gather items symbolic of increase and fertility such as crystals, herbs, seeds and fruits, flowers, and greenery. At dusk, make a large garland of the symbolic items around your bed or sacred space. Cleanse and charge the circle with apple blossom incense by wafting it clockwise around the circle with a feather or fan. Inside the garland, anoint your sacral chakra with oil. As you close your eyes, meditate on the intoxicating scent of the flowers and the fertile energy of the garland. Perform your fertility ritual, growt rite, growth spell, or divine feminine ritual. On the morning of Beltane, gather up the elements of your garland and use them to decorate your home. When the flowers and herbs have withered, gather them into a compostable bag or box and bury the box in a garden or under a fruit tree.

Note: In lieu of a large garland, you can create a floral crown and don it while you perform your rituals.

TABLETOP MAYPOLE

Symbolically represent the fertile union of energies.

Materials

Green altar cloth

Free-fallen branch from an oak, hawthorn, or rowan tree that is approximately 3 to 4 inches (8 to 10 cm) in diameter

Saw

Wood glue or screw

Anointing oils of coconut, frankincense, geranium, jasmine, and chamomile (optional)

Beltane flowers such as hawthorne, primroses, bluebells, lilac, marigolds, daisies, and lavender

Greenery

Woven willow, hazel, or apple tree twigs

Wire wrapping

Silk or linen ribbons in bright blue, green, pink, purple, and yellow

Hot glue gun (optional)

Carving knife for stripping bark

While the origin of the maypole is widely debated, it is thought by many neopagans to have been the centerpiece of an elaborate fertility rite that was held during Beltane celebrations in the Germanic regions of Europe. The pole itself—traditionally a young, sacred tree whose trunk had been cut and stripped of bark   was erected in the village green as a phallic symbol of virile male energy. It was then dressed in garlands of bright flowers, greenery, and colorful ribbons to represent the fertile female energy. On May Day, young maidens dressed in white, flowing dresses adorned with flowers danced around the pole, weaving the ribbons as they circled it in a symbolic union of the male and female energies. Lovers who had gone a-Maying the eve prior might have even joined in on the dance to ensure that their night of lovemaking had successfully resulted in conception.

In Sweden, the maypole is erected at Midsummer instead of Beltane and is called the Midsummer Pole; it has close ties to ancient fertility rites. Other traditions insist that the maypole is simply a symbol of the spring shoots that rise from the soil. While modern traditions vary based on culture and region, the maypole is still erected on May Day in many village squares and school grounds, and in folk festivals all over the world, to celebrate the blessings of the season.

Whether you plan to dance around it with friends and family or cherish it as a quiet ode to fertility and growth, the maypole deserves a position of honor amongst your sacred Beltane spaces. You can incorporate it into your main altar, erect it in the center of a fertility circle, or display it as a standalone shrine in your home or in the garden. In your chosen space, lay a green altar cloth on a solid surface that has been placed so that there is space to move around it. To construct the maypole, gather a free-fallen branch from an oak, hawthorn, or rowan tree that is approximately 3 to 4 inches (8 to 10 cm) in diameter and strip it of bark, leaves, and twigs. Using a saw, cut a 2-inch (5 cm) thick wood base from the larger end of the branch. Erect your pole by affixing the branch to the base with wood glue or a screw. If you like, anoint the length of the pole with anointing oils. Next, create a floral garland by weaving Beltane flowers and greenery through circles made of woven willow, hazel, or apple tree twigs. If need be, secure the flowers with wire wrapping. Ensure that the garland is roughly the same diameter as the top of the pole. Once the garland is complete, select silk or linen ribbons in bright colors of blue, green, pink, purple, and yellow and cut them to length; the ribbons should be at least twice the length of the pole. If you are celebrating with others, you will want to have one ribbon for each person to weave around the pole. If you will be weaving the ribbons in solitude, select one for each intention you will set. For this purpose, you may want to choose a color ribbon that corresponds to each intention; for example, green for prosperity, red for passion, and purple for spiritual enlightenment.

If you are celebrating with others, you will want to have one ribbon for each person to weave around the pole. If you will be weaving the ribbons in solitude, select one for each intention you will set. For this purpose, you may want to choose a color ribbon that corresponds to each intention; for example, green for prosperity, red for passion, and purple for spiritual enlightenment.

Tie the end of each ribbon to the garland, and affix the garland to the top of the pole with hot glue or wire wrapping. Now, you may bless the pole, play traditional fiddle or pipe music, and perform the maypole dance around your tabletop maypole as you weave the ribbons for a blessed season. Here is a May Day song that you can chant or sing while you weave the ribbons:

In light and joy, we dance 'round thee
For the blessings of growth and fertility.
Of land and self, spirit and wealth
These ribbons, we weave for perfect
    health.
Oak and hawthorne, trees of May
Gift us your baskets of flower bouquets.
Blossoming, blooming, and growing tall
'Round the Maypole we dance, one
    and all.

Note: *As an alternative to constructing your own maypole, you may use a wooden paper towel holder on which you affix ribbons with hot glue.*

POLLINATOR GARDEN

Feed the creatures of nature that are responsible for feeding us.

Materials

Tub or raised bed that can drain through the bottom

Organic, fertilized soil or soil you have fertilized yourself with compost materials or fire ash and molasses

Native wildflower seeds (see below)

Fertilizer

Watering can

Growth and beauty crystals such as green aventurine and rose quartz

Dead tree limbs

Butterfly puddler (a muddy sea salt bowl)

Bee house, bird bath, hummingbird feeder, bat box, or birdhouse (optional)

Rotting fruit (optional)

When we think of the orchards and flowers that blossom in the fertile month of May, we sometimes forget the tireless workers who ensure their fruitfulness. All fruit- and seed-bearing plants require pollination—the transfer of pollen from the male anther of the flower to the female stigma—and most do so via pollinators. Pollinators include wind, water, and animals such as birds, butterflies, bees, bats, and even flies. Attracting pollinators to our gardens is not only a metaphor for ensuring our auras are healthy and bright, but practical for ensuring the propagation of nature.

Place a tub or raised bed that can drain through the bottom in your garden or an outdoor space. Fill the space with soil. In the soil, plant a variety of native plants that will bloom from early spring to late fall so that you can provide for the pollinators throughout the seasons. Early spring bloomers include trillium, lily of the valley, daffodils, dandelions, violets, hydrangea, lupines, and irises. Summer flowers are milkweed, roses, lilies, clover, calendula, poppies, daisies, butterfly bush, bee balm, coneflower, and foxgloves. Fall bloomers include marigolds, goldenrod, asters, sunflowers, basil, borage, and lemon balm. Including night-blooming flowers such as moonflowers and evening primrose in the mix will support night flying pollinators such as bats and moths. Scatter crystals for gentle energies of growth and beauty. Along the edge of the soil, arrange dead tree limbs for larvae and bees to dwell in and a muddy sea salt bowl (known as a "butterfly puddler") for butterflies and bees. If you like, place a bee house, bird bath, hummingbird feeder, bat box, or birdhouse near the garden. You may also want to leave an offering of rotting fruit to the butterflies and flies who work so tirelessly.

FAERIE HOUSE

Ensure blessings from the fae folk for the future harvests.

Materials

Willow twigs and twine for faerie house or door

Beltane flowers such as columbines, lupines, roses, heather, foxgloves, and lily of the valley

Herbs such as thyme, vervain, and clover

Faerie crystals such as rose quartz, faerie quartz, spirit quartz, celestite, and amethyst

Honey cakes, faerie cakes, or honey-based drinks such as mead (optional)

Lilting musical instruments such as the flute, harp, or lute or music

As the first day of the Celtic summer, Beltane is a liminal time that allows magickal beings such as faeries and other folkloric creatures of nature to cross over into the human realm. According to an ancient Celtic folktale, faeries originated from the mythical race of supernatural beings that ruled early Ireland known as the Tuatha Dé Danann. Upon defeat in battle, the Tuatha shrunk themselves and fled underground. In their tunnels, they traveled from faerie village to faerie village, sometimes emerging above ground to visit their beloved Ireland once again. Faeries are said to bring much magick, joy, luck, wish-granting, prosperity, and fertility, and appeasing them with offerings of all their favorite things is a sure way to gain their blessings.

Traditionally, faerie villages are built around hawthorn trees or lone bushes, but you can begin your village in a hidden garden spot or at the base of an oak or rowan tree. Construct a house out of willow twigs by leaning them together and tying them at the top with twine. If you like, include a door or curtain at the entrance; the fae are known to enjoy their privacy. Surround your faerie house with Beltane flowers and herbs such as thyme, vervain, and clover to not only please the fae, but to woo the fae folk's beloved pollinators to their house. Decorate their "yard" with crystals such as rose quartz, faerie quartz, spirit quartz, celestite, and amethyst. If you like, bake them honey cakes or faerie cakes (tiny cupcakes that have been decorated in a whimsical style) and leave offerings of honey-based drinks such as mead outside the house. Play lilting music on the flute, harp, or lute and dance in merriment in hopes that they will join the festivities. But as you revel in the joy of the season with the fae folk, be sure to have dried rue to sprinkle around the garden as a protective ward lest the faeries' meddling turns sour and you find yourself a target of bad luck.

Note: In lieu of constructing or purchasing a faerie house, you may affix a door to the base of a tree.

CHAPTER 5

MIDSUMMER

Northern Hemisphere: June 21; Southern Hemisphere: December 21

The longest day of the year has arrived here at Midsummer with the Summer Solstice. Warm, fragrant breezes blow lazily through the sunlit fields well into the night. But just as the darkness ended, so will the light. On the Wheel of the Year, the Summer Solstice is the turning point, the point at which we begin to head into the darker half of the year. After the solstice, the days will grow shorter and the nights longer until Midwinter.

During Midsummers past, the ancient Romans celebrated the hearth goddess Vesta at her own festival, Vestalia. The ancient Egyptians welcomed the renewal of the land as the star of Sirius rose above the horizon, emerging once more from the underworld and heralding the much-anticipated annual flooding of the Nile. At the highest point in their villages, Scandinavians mimicked the retreat of the Sun by setting large wheels on fire and rolling them down hills into bodies of water. Although Midsummer is not one of the Celtic fire festivals, fire is an important component of the holiday, and hilltop bonfires on Midsummer's Eve are common even in modern celebrations. These sacred fires were thought to help the Sun reach its highest point as it teetered on the turn of the celestial wheel.

Although the holidays of Midsummer and Beltane share the pagan traditions of maypole dancing, handfasting, flower crowns, fertility rites, and faeries, Midsummer has a distinct farewell feeling to its celebrations. The growth cycle has almost completed, and the harvest is just around the corner. There is a bit of an urgency during Midsummer to relish what will soon retreat—to enjoy the long, languid days that will give way to endless hours of back-breaking work and the early arrival of nightfall. With winter preparations imminent, Midsummer stirs up a bit of carpe diem amongst young and old alike, as seen in the frolicking meadows and lusty forests of Shakespeare's *A Midsummer Night's Dream*. During this time, we honor the Sun at its peak, we ask it for healing, illumination, and one last joyful summer romp before we dip into the darkness.

LITHA ALTAR

Litha takes its name from the Anglo-Saxon words for June and July, and its altar is an ode to the powerful but dwindling sunshine that ripens the crops for the coming harvest season.

MAGICKAL CORRESPONDENCES FOR LITHA

ALTERNATIVE NAMES: Midsummer, Summer Solstice, Alban Hefin (Druidic)

COLORS: Yellow, gold, orange, red, green

CRYSTALS: Carnelian, citrine, tiger's eye, red jasper, bloodstone, copper

DEITIES: Vesta (Roman), Ra (Egyptian)

ELEMENT: Fire

FLOWERS, HERBS, AND TREES: Sunflowers, calendula, St. John's wort, lavender, rosemary, chamomile, cinnamon, frankincense, dragon's blood, clover, tiger lilies, poppies, daisies, coneflowers, black-eyed Susan, honeysuckles, goldenrod, oak, holly

FOODS: Honey, mead, summer berries, figs, peaches, nectarines

SYMBOLS: Sun wheel or Sun cross, bonfire, flower crown, candles, lanterns, Phoenix

THEMES: Celebration, folly, fire, the Sun

W hether your altar is outdoors in the fields, forest, or garden, or indoors on a sunny surface, including symbols of the Sun—bringer of warmth and light to the land—not only honors its position in the sky, but illuminates all for which you should be grateful. You can include a Norse wheel of fire as well as a golden Sun, sundial, circles, discs, and pinwheels to represent the cyclical nature of the Sun.

Fire, too, is an important element of the season. It brings passion, growth, success, creativity, motivation, and confidence. To bring the power of the flame to the Litha altar, light candles in solar colors—gold, yellow, orange, or red—and dress them with fiery herbs or oils of cinnamon, frankincense, and dragon's blood. Other lights, such as citronella candles or torches, globe or twinkle lights, or lanterns, can help to encourage the Sun on its upward journey. You may also want to include a staff with a carved Sun, lion, Phoenix, scorpion, or the alchemical symbol for the element of Fire as well as crystals such as citrine, red jasper, tiger's eye, and carnelian.

Pollinators have been busily visiting the flowers and trees of Midsummer, ensuring fruitful harvests and propagation of nature. Incorporating representations of butterflies and honeybees into your Litha altar can bring the fertility and abundance of the season into your practice. Ethically sourced and preserved specimens, artificial replicas, paintings, or pottery in a butterfly or bee theme are wonderful additions to your main altar. Include a bowl of Midsummer fruits such as strawberries, peaches, nectarines, raspberries, blueberries, apricots, or figs. Mead, a solar drink made of fermented water and honey, is often a welcome addition to the Litha altar and holiday and is considered by many to be sacred—having restorative qualities of vitality.

Whether your altar is outdoors in the fields, forest, or garden, or indoors on a sunny surface, including symbols of the Sun—bringer of warmth and light to the land—not only honors its position in the sky, but illuminates all for which you should be grateful.

If alcohol is not part of your practice, substitute a jar of solar-infused honey with Midsummer herbs such as lavender, roses, or chamomile. Wildflowers, including daisies, black-eyed Susans, lilies, coneflowers, sunflowers, and honeysuckles, and herbs such as lavender, chamomile, and St. John's wort blanket the meadows during this time of the year, so including them on your Litha altar can bring in the fertile energies of the season. Fashion them into a garland or a flower crown for maypole dancing or ritual work.

A countryside picnic feast is a popular Midsummer activity; including a basket of summer treats on your altar is an excellent way to provide a point of reflection for the bounty of the season before you head off to the meadow. Honey cakes, mead, Midsummer fruits and vegetables, fresh salads with edible weeds and flowers, and seafood are all popular choices for the Litha picnic. Summer's bounty can also make for sweet art that you can hang above your altar: Use the juice to paint symbols or scenes of the season. Many medicinal herbs are also ready for gathering at this time. Harvest basil, bay, mint, rosemary, lavender, St. John's wort, thyme, lemon balm, calendula, and sage, and solar-infuse them into oils and honeys or craft tinctures, elixirs, and oxymels to bring magickal plant vibrations to your Litha altar. It will also help fill your apothecary or medicine cabinet for the coming months when fresh herbs are scarce.

With the arrival of the Sun at its closest position comes its inevitable swing back to its farthest. Honoring this return to darkness ensures that the journey through the darker half of the year will be smooth. If you like, include symbols of the dark triumphing over light on your Litha altar. These can include the

With the arrival of the Sun at its closest position comes its inevitable swing back to its farthest. Honoring this return to darkness ensures that the journey through the darker half of the year will be smooth.

Moon eclipsing the Sun, a setting Sun, a black lace or chiffon altar cloth over a gold, yellow, orange, or red cloth, or even the elemental opposite of Fire— Water. Set out a chalice or cauldron of water in the West to douse any flames that you might light at the Litha altar to represent the dampening of Fire that accompanies the transition to Autumn.

If deities are in your practice, you may want to include a statue or altar card of the Goddess, who is now fully pregnant with the God's baby. Their love has matured and ripened, creating the stirrings of new life under the fertile Sun of Beltane. Come harvest time, the baby will be born and the God will give his life as the reaping of the fields begins.

The solstice also brings the folkloric defeat of the Oak King. The Holly King has triumphed and is ready to take his seat on the throne. Honor each by including oak leaves, branches, and acorns for the dethroned Oak King and mistletoe or holly for the newly reigning Holly King. Sun gods and goddesses such as Áine (Celtic goddess of summer), Belenus (Celtic Sun god), Sol (Norse Sun goddess), and Ra (Egyptian Sun god) can also be honored on the Litha altar.

OAK TREE SHRINE

Bid farewell to the lighter half of the year and the reign of the Oak King.

Materials

Stool, tree stump, chair, or table (optional)

Green altar cloth

Acorns and oak leaves

Oak bowls (optional)

Chalice of wine or water

Symbols of fertility, creativity, life, wealth, wisdom, protection, and growth

Statue of the Oak King (optional)

An oak tree shrine is a fond farewell to the reign of summer. As the most prevalent tree in the ancient forests of England, the oak tree has long been venerated there. Thought to be the first sacred tree of the Druids, the oak represents all that Midsummer celebrates: fertility, creativity, health, success, and strength. Aside from its ties to immortality and life itself, the oak tree is also a powerful protector, and those who evoke the mighty oak will be safe from negative energies. If you have been following the saga of the Oak and Holly Kings, it is at this time that the Holly King comes to claim his rightful throne.

Though the branches of the oak are green with growth and heavy with acorns, they will soon litter the ground below.

Create your shrine at the base of an oak tree or on a pedestal underneath its canopy. The pedestal can be a stool, tree stump, table, or a chair on which you lay a green altar cloth. You may also use the lush summer grass or a bed of moss as your foundation. Gather acorns and leaves from the tree and scatter them around the shrine or offer them in bowls made of oak. As a sign of gratitude, offer a chalice of wine or water in the elemental western direction of Water. You may also include symbols of fertility, creativity, life, wealth, wisdom, protection, and growth as well as a statue of the Oak King. Every time you stop at the shrine, you can honor the mighty oak by gifting more acorns and pouring more wine, asking for nothing in return other than its blessings for the season.

Note: *In lieu of creating this shrine under an oak tree, you may mount a fallen oak branch or twig with the leaves still attached on your wall. If you must cut the branch, be sure the tree is healthy and that you leave it an offering as a sign of your gratitude.*

SACRED PICNIC SPACE

Celebrate the foods and merriment of Midsummer.

Materials

Picnic blanket in a solar color such as red, yellow, or gold

Candles

Summer flowers

Gold plate or round tray

Greenery

Fiery incense such as sandalwood or frankincense

Cast-iron pot

Summery potpourri blend: chamomile, calendula, sunflower petals, St. John's wort, coneflower, lemon balm, and orange slices or peel

Picnic basket of feast foods: Sun tea with lemon, freshly pressed juice, honey cakes, crispbread or crusty breads, summer berries, watermelon slices, strawberry pie, pickled or cured fish, smoked sausage, new potato salad with mustard and dill, and a salad with fresh greens and edible flowers such as lavender, nasturtiums, squash, chives, basil, roses, and sunflowers

Wine, ale, juice, or mead (optional)

Countryside picnics are a staple of many Midsummer festivals during which most of the celebrations take place outdoors. This way, modern pagans enjoy the longest day of the year in the same way ancient pagans did—with light-hearted and festive merriment. In Sweden, the Midsummer picnic is an esteemed part of the celebrations, and a smorgasbord of summer foods is enjoyed. Freshly picked fruits and vegetables, herring, summer sausages, and crispbread are spread out on blankets in forests and fields while the festivities of Midsummer abound. Dancing, music, flower crowns, sunbathing, swimming, and rituals for growth and fertility are often performed around the Midsummer feast.

You may choose to hold your picnic in the woods under an oak tree, atop a hill, on a beach or river bank, in the middle of a meadow, or even at a sunny breakfast nook in your home—whatever brings the vitality and sunshine of Midsummer to your feast. Facing the East with the Sun's growing energy, lay a picnic blanket in a solar color on the ground. Make a centerpiece of candles and flowers on a golden plate or round tray to symbolize the abundant fertility and gratitude for the Sun at the pinnacle of its cycle. Decorate the picnic space with greenery and burn fiery incense. In a cast-iron pot, simmer a potpourri blend of chamomile, calendula, sunflower petals, St. John's wort, coneflower, lemon balm, and orange slices or peel. Unpack your picnic basket for a feast that can be set out and enjoyed all afternoon. You may also include wine, ale, juice, and mead. While enjoying your picnic feast, prepare two small plates for offerings to both the faeries and the woodland creatures.

SOLAR CHARGING ALTAR

Cleanse and charge your magickal tools with the most powerful Sun of the year.

Materials

Gold or yellow candle in a glass bowl (optional)

Your magickal tools, such as anointing oils, flower and herbal blends, crystals, candles, staffs, wands, and even food or drink

Glass bowls or dishes to hold your magickal tools

White altar cloth

Card of gratitude (optional)

Oak leaves (optional)

Honey (optional)

The Sun shines brightly on the solstice, stretching its rays across the land from its perch on the cycle's peak. This powerful day is perfect for retuning your magickal tools and rituals items to their natural frequencies. When we use magickal tools such as crystals and wands in our rituals and spells, we alter their natural frequency state in favor of our intentions. To keep our crystals in tip-top shape, we must treat them as we would any other trade tools—by cleansing them of accumulated vibrational dust and charging them with energy. Although there are many ways to cleanse and charge magickal tools, sunlight is potent, abundant, and, best of all, free.

This altar should be created either outside or in an indoor space that receives direct sunlight. If this is not possible, you may use a solar representation such as a gold or yellow candle in a glass bowl. Consider placing the charging space in a well-trafficked spot, as you will likely want to visit it many times throughout the festivities to gather tools for your rituals. These tools could include anointing oils, flower and herbal blends, crystals, candles, staffs or wands, or even food and drink. With this altar, you are inviting the Sun to exude its full power upon your tools, so use only a simple display of glass bowls or dishes and a white altar cloth to ensure the rays are directed at their intention. If you like, write a saying of gratitude on a card to thank the Sun for its hard work, and set up an offering of oak leaves and honey alongside the altar.

Note: *Keep in mind that there are some crystals that should not be placed in direct sunlight because they will fade or become brittle over time. These are usually semitransparent crystals such as amethyst, fluorite, citrine, celestite, rose quartz, and smoky quartz. Also be aware that some faceted crystals and spheres could direct magnified and focused sunlight onto a single spot and cause a fire.*

HEALING ALTAR

Call forth the healing powers of the Sun.

Materials

Wooden round or gold plate

**Jar of naturally sourced
or purified water**

**Bowls of healing herbs such as
chamomile, echinacea, ginseng,
agrimony, turmeric, milk thistle,
dandelion, calendula, St. John's wort,
and feverfew**

Chamomile and calendula (optional)

**Crystals such as citrine or amber
for amulet**

Gold or yellow cloth

Candles in solar colors

**Midsummer flowers, such as
sunflowers, calendula, poppies,
roses, tiger lilies, dandelions,
and daisies**

Sun gong

The rays of the Sun are a life-sustaining force that can mend both the body and spirit. In ancient times, solar deities were worshipped for their healing powers. The ancient Celtic god Belenus could melt away sickness, and the Roman Sun god, Apollo, could cure disease. Even in modern times, doctors and healers use the Sun to mend wounds and treat diseases such as rickets, jaundice, and tuberculosis. Yogis, too, prescribe sun-gazing as a potent healing force—the *pranayama* (or breath of fire) is thought to connect the practitioner with the energy of the Sun and the element of Fire, thereby cleansing the body of toxins and purifying the spirit.

Healing is a personal journey, and your altar space should reflect that. If you enjoy a direct spot in the Sun, choose that. But if your solace is indoors away from the noise and chaos of the world, then find a sunny spot in your favorite room. Situate your altar so that it is facing the direction of the rising Sun. Using a wooden round or a golden plate as your altar base, place a jar of naturally sourced or purified water in direct sunlight and allow it to charge as the Sun rises to its highest point of the year. Place bowls of healing herbs around the jar. If you like, make a soothing decoction of chamomile and calendula by infusing them into your water. Create a healing amulet by charging a piece of citrine or amber on the wooden round under a gold or yellow cloth. Surround the wooden round with solar-colored candles and Midsummer flowers as offerings to the Sun. When the Sun reaches high noon, you may call its energy to your healing altar by ringing a Sun gong or another instrument that is tuned to the frequency of the Sun.

WITCH BEACH BOTTLE

Cast off negative or toxic energies.

Materials

Glass or ceramic bottle with cork

Found beach items such as sand, shells, stones, feathers, flowers, and sea glass

Sea water or water and sea salt

Parchment paper and pen

Wax seal

The beach has long been a place of worship and captivation. At this transitional boundary, where the land meets the sea, we can imbue magickal tools such as spell bottles with immense power. Spell bottles, also known as *witch bottles*, were used in olden times to protect against witchcraft. They were filled with urine, blood, rusty nails, thorns, and needles and then hidden in the barns. It was thought that as long as the witch bottle remained whole, the witch could not cause any harm. Modern practitioners have since reclaimed witch bottles to counter psychic attacks and ward off harmful intentions. Though the Midsummer Sun is a bringer of life and joy, too much fire can quickly spread beyond control. This witch bottle protects against the careless heat of the solstice Sun and dampens the wildfires that rage within

Select a corked glass or ceramic bottle. Visit the sea or a natural water source and collect things such as sand, shells, stones, feathers, flowers, and sea glass, saying a small protective chant over each one as you place them gently in the bottle: "With the sea, dampen the fire within me." Once you have collected everything that speaks to you, fill the bottle with sea water. If you do not have sea water, sprinkle a bit of sea salt into the mix. On a piece of parchment, you may write a protection sigil or symbol like an eye of Horus or Mjolnir (Thor's Hammer), an intention, or something you would like to leave buried in the salty sea. Perhaps a fire rages within you or something threatens to combust at any moment: anger, obsession, or addiction, for example. Any of these strong emotions or feelings are attributed to the Fire element and can be dampened by Water. Roll up the parchment and slide it inside your bottle. Seal the bottle with the cork and a melted wax seal. Now, at sunset on the solstice, throw your witch bottle onto the sacred flames of your Litha bonfire. When it bursts, it drowns the flames within you and signals the death of the Sun.

WAKE FOR THE SUN

Celebrate the growth you have achieved and bid farewell to all that has held you back.

Materials

Yellow or gold tablecloth

Summer flowers and greenery

Lights

4 white candles

Clock

Musical instruments such as pipes and flutes

Midsummer picnic leftovers or other feast foods (such as summer punch and berry cake)

Gold or yellow dinnerware

Midsummer flower petals or seeds

Piece of rotting fruit

The Summer Solstice pays homage not only to the Sun's highest point in the sky but to its impending death as it retreats into the darker half of the year. During this time, amidst celebratory fire rituals and Midsummer picnics, we bid the fiery wheel a fond farewell. Although many ancient pagans practiced funeral rites in celebration of their dead, none lend themselves to the Wheel of the Year quite as definitively as the Irish wake. The Irish wake, still practiced today, is a well-known Irish custom of "waking the dead" so that they may mingle with the living once

more before passing on. A wake for the Sun allows us to prepare for the coming darkness while sending the Sun on its journey.

Set up a large table outside, in the "house" of the dying Sun. Lay down a yellow or gold tablecloth, and decorate it with symbols of the Sun such as gold discs, plates, or castings along with summer flowers, greenery, and lights. At each of the four corners of the table, place a white candle. Include a clock that has been symbolically "frozen" at the time of your region's sunset on the solstice to represent the Sun's impending death. To represent the traditional keeners who wail symbolically at Irish wakes, include musical instruments such as pipes or flutes. Finally, arrange your evening feast around the table. You can include many of the same foods from your Midsummer picnic or just dress up the leftovers with gold or yellow dinnerware as well as a summer punch and berry cake to round out the meal.

This is also a wake for yourself—a celebration of all your growth and a farewell to all that has held you back. Write a word or two of your good deeds in Midsummer flower petals or seeds and let the wind scatter them. On a piece of rotting fruit, write something of which you would like to let go. Later, deeply bury it in the hardening soil. Perhaps something wonderful will grow in its place.

CHAPTER 6

LUGHNASADH

Northern Hemisphere: August 1; Southern Hemisphere: February 1

The gateway to the darker half of the year, Lughnasadh is the cross-quarter holiday between Midsummer and the Autumn Equinox and the first of the three harvest festivals on the Wheel of the Year. Also called the First Harvest, it is a grain festival commonly held across northern Europe. It celebrates the first reaping of wheat. *Lughnasadh* translates to "Commemoration of Lugh" in Irish Gaelic and is thought to originally have been a Celtic funeral feast for the Sun god Lugh. According to Irish mythology, Lugh held athletic games, markets, and feasts in honor of his foster mother, who died of exhaustion after clearing the fields of Ireland for agriculture. Although Lughnasadh is sometimes referred to as *Lammas* (or loaf-mass) by modern pagans, Lammas is a Christian holiday into which the traditions of Lughnasadh were adopted, much like Candlemas and Hallowmas. During Lammastide, the Anglo-Saxons presented loaves of bread made from freshly harvested wheat to the church for blessing. Once consecrated, the loaves might have been broken up into four pieces and the pieces placed in each corner of the barn to protect the harvested grain from mice and other pests.

In modern paganism, the First Harvest festival is often celebrated as a blend of the Anglo-Saxon Lammas and the Celtic Lughnasadh traditions. It is a time to gather with friends and family and begin the difficult work of harvesting all that we have sown since the beginning of spring. The first sheaves of grain are cut and made into bread; the transformation from toil to sustenance is complete. Lughnasadh is a time of abundance but also a time of preparation as we begin the transition into the darker, scanter time of year. Grain, itself a symbol of the cycle of life, is not only stored as food, but saved as seed to be planted once again come spring.

LUGHNASADH ALTAR

The Lughnasadh altar is golden and ripe with the bounty of the First Harvest: grains such as wheat, oats, barley, and corn; fruit such as berries, grapes, apples, plums, and peaches; and vegetables such as squash and pumpkins.

MAGICKAL CORRESPONDENCES OF LUGHNASADH

ALTERNATIVE NAMES: Lammas/ Hlaefmass/Loafmass (Anglo-Saxon), Gwyl Awst (Welsh), First Harvest, Grain Harvest

COLORS: Yellow, gold, orange, green, brown

CRYSTALS: Citrine, red jasper, carnelian, tiger's eye, peridot, topaz

DEITIES: Lugh (Celtic), Ceres (Roman), Persephone/Kore (Greek), Demeter (Greek), John Barleycorn (Celtic)

ELEMENT: Fire/Water

FLOWERS, HERBS, AND TREES: Wheat, barley, corn, oats, sunflowers, meadowsweet, mint, calendula, blackthorn, elder, hops, crab apples, berries, grapes

FOODS: Grains, bread, berries, ale, wine, jam, barley cakes, apples, bilberries, squash, colcannon

SYMBOLS: Corn, sunflowers, agricultural tools (sickle, scythe, or boline), cauldron or chalice

THEMES: Harvest, abundance, prosperity, purification, preparation, transformation, death

In a sunny spot on an indoor table, lay down an altar cloth in the muted green of the late summer grass or the golden yellow of the grain in the fields and decorate it with cornstalks, corn cobs, wheat sheaves, green garlands, and late flowers such as sunflowers and calendula. Weave in early harvest colors such as gold, yellow, red, green, brown, and orange with candles and bowls or plates to contain loose grains or bread. Include a wreath made from garlic or a Sun wheel or pentacle formed from softened wheat stalks to represent the dying Sun. Burn seasonal incense and herbs such as frankincense, apple blossoms, patchouli, lavender, and cinnamon in a small pot. Scatter crystals that assist with creativity and manifestation, or store energy for the lean times to come; they could include citrine, red jasper, carnelian, tiger's eye, and quartz generators. Agricultural tools, too, can be included to symbolize the harvest—sickles, scythes, woven baskets, and twine for binding are all used to reap what we have sown. Even in this time of great abundance, they beg the question: Did we prepare enough? Are there projects or intentions that need to be wrapped up before winter sets in? Is there anything else we would like to begin before the harvest comes to an end?

During the First Harvest, the folkloric John Barleycorn (also known as the God of the Harvest, Lugh, and the Green Man in his dying aspect) sacrifices his life so that humankind can survive the winter. In remembrance of all that he has sacrificed, coneflowers and poppies are often placed on the altar. Once the First Harvest has been completed, the spirit of the Corn Mother (also known as the Goddess, Grain Mother, and Harvest Queen) is preserved in a corn dolly made from the last sheaf cut. The dolly is kept in the home over the winter, where it acts as a

Including symbolic kitchen tools and ingredients on your main altar can remind you that the abundance of the season is fleeting and will need transformation if it is to sustain you over winter.

charm of protection. In North American pagan traditions, corn husk dolls are often made in the likeness of those that originated with ancient Native American spiritual practices, which were later adopted by early European settlers. To represent the spirit of the grain on your altar, you may create a wheat or corn husk dolly or decorate the space with dried husks, flint corn, or wheat sheaves.

The Lughnasadh feast is an important aspect of the holiday and should have its own sacred spread in your home. Including symbolic kitchen tools and ingredients on your main altar can remind you that the abundance of the season is fleeting and will need transformation if it is to sustain you over winter. Feature a mortar and pestle, measuring spoons, herbs and spices, salt and pepper grinders, vinegars and oils, or canning and jarring equipment. Bowls or jars of seeds or grains alongside a fresh loaf of bread can help you focus on the preparations at hand.

Although Lughnasdh is one of the four Celtic fire festivals, the bonfires that litter the hilltops of the other cross-quarter holidays are not as prevalent during the modern celebrations of this holiday, perhaps because of the intense heat that late summer already brings to the land. Here, you may use the Fire element symbolically to represent purification and transformation. Pillar or beeswax candles in the colors of the harvest can bring the energy needed to your altar. Anointing oils made from herbs and extracts of cayenne, St. John's wort,

If deities are in your practice, you might consider honoring the Celtic god after which the holiday is named: Lugh was a skilled craftsman and considered by many to be the "artisan god of the Celts."

calendula, sunflowers, nettle, cinnamon, bay, and saffron can light the fire underneath you, too. If you would like to take part in the traditional fire purification rites, burn loose incense of meadowsweet and mugwort on the altar and pass your magickal tools through the smoke.

If deities are in your practice, you might consider honoring the Celtic god after which the holiday is named: Lugh was a skilled craftsman and considered by many to be the "artisan god of the Celts." His talents are said to spread far and wide and include smithcraft, music, art, athleticism, and poetry. By honoring him or making offerings to him at your altar, you can ask that he bestow his mastery and determination on you. Or, you may want to honor your own talents or trade (or a trade that you would like to develop) with symbolic tools for such skills as blacksmithing, writing, sewing, knitting, glassblowing, pottery, jewelry-making, or witchcraft-minded skills such as tarot. Craft festivals are common at this time of year, after all. Including your finished wares on the altar honors the cycle of your craft and the work you put into it.

ORCHARD SEAT

Set intentions that will grow with the harvests of autumn.

Materials

Small table

Paper and pen

Pillar candle in a color that corresponds to your intention (see below)

Carving knife

Anointing oil: dried apple blossoms and seeds and sweet almond oil

Apple

Knife

Crystals that relate to your intention, plus crystals for personal growth such as citrine and jade

Apple blossom incense

Small fireproof dish

During the month of August, the delicate apple blossoms of spring give way to clusters of ripening fruit. The crabapple was first domesticated thousands of years ago and, through cultivation and distribution, evolved into the many varieties of apples that fill market shelves today. In ancient Germanic, Celtic, and Anglo-Saxon regions, crabapples were symbols of everlasting life and an important source of cider production. From the perseverance of the seeds through the harshness of winter, to the fertile blossoms unfurling with possibility in the spring, to the apple itself providing sustenance come harvest, the apple has rightly earned its title as the "fruit of the gods." In Greek mythology, the immortal apple binds Persephone, the Greek goddess of grain, to the Underworld during winter. In Christianity, this "forbidden fruit" contains all the knowledge of good and evil. And in modern paganism, the apple is the perfect balance of the elements and a symbol of the growth cycle.

Place a small table under the canopy of an apple tree (or branch) that is in good health and has a history of successful harvests. Decide on an intention you wish to grow, and write it down on a piece of paper. Apples are excellent allies for fertility and love, wisdom and creativity, and realm travel and ancestral work. Choose a symbol to represent your intention and carve it into a pillar candle of a corresponding color (for example, a heart on a pink candle for self-love). Create an anointing oil for the candle by infusing dried apple blossoms and seeds into sweet almond oil. Cut an apple in half horizontally and display the pentagram of seeds. Include crystals for your specific intention as well as those used for personal growth such as citrine and jade. Burn apple blossom incense in a small fireproof dish and begin your ritual work. Under this tree, your intention will be protected as it grows, but always remember: Whatever is begun under an apple tree will only be as fruitful as the tree itself.

SKILLS ALTAR

Honor and nurture your skills and talents.

Materials

Green pillar or taper candles

Elemental crystals: carnelian, amethyst, blue kyanite, and green aventurine

Potted summer herbs such as lavender for clarity or sage for success, or botanical sprays

Symbols of your work (see below)

Infused water or tea

In Irish mythology, Lugh approached the Tuatha Dé Danann and insisted that there was no one with as many skills as he and that he should therefore be granted admittance. He was appointed to the court of King Nuada and, shortly thereafter, given command of the Tuatha Dé Danann in battle. Legend has it that Lugh was not only a fierce warrior and athletic contender, but a talented blacksmith, artisan, sorcerer, bard, historian, and physician, amongst other things. The name given to him by the Dananns was *Samildanach*, or "the Many-Skilled God."

Although the sacred space under an apple tree is an ideal place to perform a growth ritual, this altar is a place to actually do the work. It is best to create it on your worktable or desk, where you will have access to your tools. Place a green pillar or taper candle on either side of the work surface, and place crystals for each element in their cardinal directions: carnelian for courage in the West, amethyst for focus in the East, blue kyanite for balance in the South, and green aventurine for growth in the North. Include potted summer herbs such as lavender for clarity and sage for success or a botanical spray for cleansing the space and inviting in fresh energy. Now, focus the remaining components of the altar on your skill. If you are a writer, for example, you may create this altar on your desk and include a computer or typewriter as well as a notebook and pen. Perhaps a tea kettle with orange peel and lemon balm will provide clarity and stimulation for conjuring fresh ideas. If your workspace is at the forge, however, you may want to include a forged item that is of particular importance to you or at a level of mastery to which you aspire. Perhaps you would also like to display the rune Berkana for continued growth and rebirth. Include a lemon balm–infused face mister to cool the fiery energy of the forge.

HARVEST SPIRIT SHRINE

Symbolically represent the harvest cycle.

Materials

Wooden round or gold tray

Green altar cloth

Bread dough to shape into a bread-man loaf

Disc-shaped edible eyes, seeds, leaf-shapes, and edible flowers to decorate the bread-man

Stems of dried wheat sheaves or corn husks to make into corn dolly (try Simply Straw if you cannot find this locally)

In mythology, gods and goddesses were often immortalized in the Earth's cycles. The grain of the First Harvest is no different. The god Lugh is represented as John Barleycorn (or the Green Man) and resides as a spirit in the corn. When the grain is cut, so is his time here in the Earthly realm. His spirit is preserved in the loaf of bread made from the first sheaf of the wheat harvest and reborn as the seeds that will be sown come spring. He has given his life to nourish others. This concept is, in many ways, symbolic of the spirit of the First Harvest: For the cycle to continue, there must be death. The Goddess (or Grain Mother), who in Greek mythology is known as Demeter, is represented as the corn. Her daughter, often personified as Persephone, is the seed. And just as the Goddess gave birth to the seed, the seed will give birth come spring. Although the first sheaf is thought to contain the spirit of the God, it is the last sheaf that contains the spirit of the Goddess. A corn dolly or grain mother is made from this last sheaf and is thought to preserve and protect the spirit of the Goddess. It is housed at the hearth or above the door, where it will protect the home and its occupants until spring. Come planting time, it will be plowed into the first furrow so that it may fertilize the spirit of John Barleycorn.

A corn dolly or grain mother is made from this last sheaf and is thought to preserve and protect the spirit of the Goddess. It is housed at the hearth or above the door, where it will protect the home and its occupants until spring.

On a simple indoor foundation—ideally the hearth, fireplace mantle, or a shelf above the front door—place a wooden round or a gold tray and a green altar cloth. To represent the god, make a loaf of bread in the traditional figure of John Barleycorn known as a "bread-man." You may decorate it with disc-shaped eyes for the Sun, as well as with seeds, leaf-shapes, and edible flowers. As an alternative to the bread-man, you can make a plaited loaf of bread or a wreath to symbolize the harvest. As you work the bread, enchant it with a small blessing, something like "From seed to harvest to nourish the land and around the Wheel to grow again." Scottish poet Robert Burns published a poem about John Barleycorn in the eighteenth century that was later made into a folk song. It symbolizes the cycle of life of the grain spirit. You may want to write it down or include a printout of it on your spirit shrine. It begins like this:

> There was three kings into the east,
> Three kings both great and high,
> And they hae sworn a solemn oath
> John Barleycorn should die.
>
> They took a plough and plough'd
>   him down,
> Put clods upon his head,
> And they hae sworn a solemn oath
> John Barleycorn was dead.
>
> But the cheerful Spring came kindly on,
> And show'rs began to fall;
> John Barleycorn got up again,
> And sore surpris'd them all.

In Native American traditions, the dolls are made from husks of corn. There are many legends of the corn husk doll, and they vary by tribe, but the "no-face dolls" are typically crafted in ceremony as a lesson to teach the young to be humble.

To represent the goddess, make a corn dolly. The corn dolly (also known as a corn maiden, corn mother, or corn husk doll) is a poppet of sympathetic magic that is created to house the corn spirit during the winter while the land rests. It can often take a human shape (usually the shape of a female), but it can also be in a plait, besom, cross, spiral, pentacle, heart, or any other shape that is symbolic of the season. To create your own corn dolly, first hollow the stems of wheat sheaves or source them from somewhere like Simply Straw. Soak them in warm water until they are pliable. Then, you may plait them into any shape you like, or simply just bind them in the center so that they can stand on their own. It is traditional to leave a space inside the torso of the doll for the grain spirit to reside. In Native American traditions, the dolls are made from husks of corn. There are many legends of the corn husk doll, and they vary by tribe, but the "no-face dolls" are typically crafted in ceremony as a lesson to teach the young to be humble. This indigenous practice of corn husk doll–making was adopted by European colonists and has since found its way to modern paganism

SACRED BAKING SPACE

Imbue the feast foods of the First Harvest with magick and intention.

Materials

Butcher block or large cutting board

**Candles in the colors of the First Harvest,
such as gold, yellow, brown, or orange**

**Symbol of Lugh's talents, such as
a spear or a slingshot (optional)**

Jars or bowls of ingredients

Canning and baking tools

Grains

Yeast

Cast-iron pot

Measuring cup of water or milk

Sage or rosemary incense

**Flour mixed with Lughnasadh herbs,
such as mint and calendula**

**Festive apron in harvest colors
(optional)**

The heart of baking lies in transformation.
From seed, we grow wheat, which stands tall
and golden in the fields. We mill the wheat
and mix the flour with yeast and ask it to rise
into bread, which will fill our bellies and feed
our spirits. Barley is fermented into ale, berries are preserved in jams, and late summer
herbs are infused into oil, all so that we may
be sustained over the long winter. During
the feast of Lughnasadh, it is traditional to
share the transformation of our harvest with
those around us. Community bread is baked
not only as a symbol of the preservation of
the corn spirit, but as a gesture of goodwill
and gratitude for all that has been bestowed
upon us.

The sacred baking space of the first harvest
will be a working altar, so it is best to create it
on a butcher block countertop or large cutting
board. Once you have cleaned your surface,
place candles in the colors of the First
Harvest around your workspace. If you like,
include one candle each for John Barleycorn
and the Grain Mother. If deities are in your
practice, call Lugh to the altar by including
a symbol of one of his many talents. Around
your workspace, organize your ingredients
in jars or bowls, as well as your canning and
baking tools. Call the elements to the altar by
placing grains in the North, yeast (with its
rising bubbles) in the East, a cast-iron pot in
the South, and a measuring cup of water or
milk in the West. Energetically cleanse and
bless your tools and ingredients with sage
or rosemary incense and sprinkle a bit of
flour that you have mixed with the herbs of
Lughnasadh over your surface to consecrate
your workspace. If you like, select a festive
apron in the colors of the season to bring a bit
of the First Harvest magick to your wardrobe.

FEAST TABLE ALTAR

Share the feast foods of the First Harvest with your village of family and friends.

Materials

Picnic blanket in First Harvest colors

Greenery and herbs such as rosemary, mint, and meadowsweet garlands

Candles in the colors of the season

Feast foods such as freshly baked breads, berry pies, and tarts; berry jam or elderberry wine; basil pesto, garlic butter, and herbed leeks; pumpkins, squash, potatoes, cabbage, corn on the cob, and other late summer vegetables

According to Irish mythology, Lughnasadh commemorates the funeral feast that Lugh held for his foster mother, Tailtiu. The feast was a time for the people of Ireland to come together and express their gratitude for the work that she had done in the fields. On the feast table, the grain underwent a complete transformation, and the communal loaves of bread were a symbolic representation of the harvest cycle. On Bilberry Sunday, great treks to the mountain tops were made to pick bilberries, small blueberry-like berries that grow in Great Britain and Northern Europe. Colcannon, a traditional Irish meal of mashed potatoes and cabbage, was also a welcome addition to the Lughnasadh table.

Because the abundance of the First Harvest feast is a reminder of the hard work that has been done, athleticism was also an important part of the Lughnasadh feast. The Tailteann Games tested vim and vigor and included such activities as chariot racing, spear throwing, and archery.

The feast of the grain harvest celebrates the transformation that the fruits of our labor has undergone. Although this feast is about sustenance, it is also about preparation, and you will notice that many of the recipes call for items that can be stored in the winter. Choose a feast location with wide open spaces to accommodate your community as well as any Tailteann-like games you might play—a park, a field, or your backyard. Set up a table or a picnic blanket in First Harvest colors, and decorate it with greenery and herbs like rosemary, mint, and meadowsweet garlands as well as candles in the colors of the season. For the feast, bake loaves of bread, berry pies, and tarts. Open a jar of berry jam or a bottle of elderberry wine. From the last of the fresh green harvest, make basil pesto, garlic butter, and herbed leeks. Pumpkins, squash, potatoes, cabbage, corn on the cob, and the other late summer vegetables are wonderfully festive to display and eat.

CHAPTER 7
AUTUMN EQUINOX

Northern Hemisphere: September 21; Southern Hemisphere: March 21

The Autumn Equinox brings night and day into equal length once again. This time, though, the balance hangs on the death of the Sun as it moves toward its winter position. From here on, each night will stretch its inky shadow over more of the daylight until we cycle around to the Winter Solstice once again. The Autumn Equinox is the official start of fall and the second of three harvest festivals on the Wheel of the Year. The Full Moon nearest the equinox is known as the Harvest Moon, because it allows farmers to work through the night, harvesting their crops under its illumination. The Druids celebrated the feast of the Autumn Equinox as Alban Elfed while the Christians honor Saint Michael, the patron saint of sailors and slayer of dragons, on Michaelmas. In China during an annual Moon Festival, lanterns are hung, mooncakes are served, and offerings are made to the Moon in gratitude for a successful harvest of rice and wheat. Cosmically, the Autumn Equinox is the time of year when the geomagnetic storms in Earth's atmosphere are strongest and give rise to astounding views of the Northern Lights.

In modern paganism, the Autumnal Equinox is often celebrated as the holiday known as Mabon. Known colloquially as the "Witches' Thanksgiving," Mabon is a modern pagan reconstruction of Second Harvest traditions and includes early fall activities such as communal feasting. In the spirit of giving thanks, Mabon festivalgoers gather at great tables and halls to delight in the foods of the season and honor the importance of community. With the horn o' plenty at the center of the table, they celebrate the abundance of the season before the lean times arrive. During Mabon, we not only hope for a blessed and continued harvest, but we honor the balance of light and dark and the transition to the fall season

MABON ALTAR

The Mabon altar is rich with the grains and fruits that are reaped at the end of the Second Harvest season. Corn and wheat, root vegetables, gourds, nuts, berries, grapes, and fruit are plucked from the fields and orchards as the crops give in to the dying of the Sun.

MAGICKAL CORRESPONDENCES OF MABON

ALTERNATIVE NAMES: Autumn Equinox, Fall Equinox, Second Harvest, Alban Elfed (Druidic), Michaelmas (Christian), Witches' Thanksgiving

COLORS: Burgundy, eggplant, gold, burnt orange, chocolate brown, dark red, indigo

CRYSTALS: Orange calcite, carnelian, tiger's eye, topaz, amber, lapis lazuli

DEITIES: Gaia (Greek), Demeter (Greek), Ma'at (Egyptian), Adrestia (Greek), Pamona (Roman), Mabon ap Modron (Welsh), Bacchus (Greek)

ELEMENT: Water

FLOWERS, HERBS, AND TREES: Saffron, rue, marigold, vines, ivy, hops, grape leaves, burdock, goldenrod, cattails, oak, rowan, myrrh, frankincense, amyris, benzoin, patchouli, cinnamon, sage, cloves

FOODS: Pomegranates, grapes, apples, root vegetables, potatoes, stews, nuts, corn, berries, wine, ale, cider

SYMBOLS: Skulls, acorns, pinecones, cornucopia, autumn leaves, grapevines, gourds, vines

THEMES: Equality, balance, harvest, harmony, abundance, protection, death

These bountiful harvests can adorn the feast table's natural wooden surface of deep mahogany or rich maple. Farming tools such as blades, sickles, scythes, and cornucopia baskets can be placed in the center on a golden plate or tray. They gracefully request gratitude for the abundance of the season. Candles in the colors of the season, rich plums and burgundies accented with bright golds and deep browns, can be lit to remind us that there is light to be found even in growing darkness.

As the autumn winds blow, they carry leaves in vibrant shades of red, orange, and yellow. Drying the leaves and scattering them along the feast table altar serves as a reminder that while the Earth is preparing for slumber, we must prepare for the barren months ahead. What cannot be eaten during the feast or stored in the root cellar must be preserved for winter. A flurry of canning and pickling, along with cider-, beer-, and winemaking, often accompanies the Second Harvest. Including jams and other canned or jarred goods in the feast represents the necessity of transforming the fruits of our labor. Leaving a glass or drinking horn of a freshly brewed drink such as wine or cider on the Mabon altar is an offering to the season—a gift to nature for bestowing upon us the ingredients for transformation. Apples, too, can be cut in half horizontally so that the pentagram of seeds calls upon all the elements of nature in balance.

This balance is also reflected in the equality of night and day that the equinox brings. During this time, our shadow self, the part of us that holds our darkest desires, should be brought into the light once again and integrated into our conscious self so that we may embark on our journey to becoming whole. Adorning the Mabon altar with symbols of this balance between light and dark—such as black and white candle pairs, the yin and yang symbol, and the Sun and Moon—can help bring focus to this intention. You may also write your

Candles in the colors of the season, rich plums and burgundies accented with bright golds and deep browns, can be lit to remind us that there is light to be found even in growing darkness.

intentions on bay leaves and burn them in a fireproof pot containing herbs and resins of Mabon, which include sage and myrrh.

Although Samhain is widely considered to be the festival on which we commune with the dead, Mabon is the time to begin rekindling our relationships with those who have passed. To invite them to take part in the offerings of your celebratory feast (and to ensure that they are pleased with your remembrances come Samhain), you can place mementos or photos of your dearly departed on the Mabon altar. Light a white taper candle in front of each to acknowledge their strengthening presence. Then, they will bring only kindness and good fortune across the veil.

If deities are in your practice, you can display statues, altar cards, or symbolic items of the gods and goddesses of Mabon. Although Mabon is celebrated across many modern pagan traditions, it is thought that the celebration itself is a reconstruction of ancient Celtic traditions that took place around the time of the equinox. The name *Mabon* comes from the Welsh Sun god, Child of Light, and son of the Earth Mother (Modron). Calling upon the "Great Son of the Great Mother" can bring the cyclical concept

Although Samhain is widely considered to be the festival on which we commune with the dead, Mabon is the time to begin rekindling our relationships with those who have passed.

of death and rebirth to the Mabon altar. In Greek mythology, Demeter, or the Dark Mother of Winter, is often offered wine; it is on this day each year that her daughter Persephone returns to the underworld to live with her husband, Hades, until Spring. Hecate, the Greek Goddess of witchcraft; Dionysus, the Greek god of wine and resurrection; Bacchus, the Roman equivalent of Dionysus; and the Wiccan Oak and Holly Kings can also be honored on the Mabon altar. The Goddess is in her crone aspect as the Dark Mother or Harvest Queen. The God is dead, imprisoned in the underworld until spring, when he will be reborn.

After the great feast has ended and the equinox has passed, it is customary to offer the harvest remains of the Mabon altar to the animals that share your land. Leave a small plate or bowl filled with leftover fruits, berries, and nuts outside on the edge of the forest or at the base of a tree for squirrels, deer, birds, and other creatures who are busily preparing for the long winter ahead to enjoy.

CORNUCOPIA OFFERING

Honor the abundance of the Second Harvest.

Materials

Altar cloth in the colors of the Second Harvest, such as burgundy, gold, or chocolate brown

Dried autumn leaves and corn cobs

Self-standing gourds

Anointing oil: olive oil infused with herbs such as sage, rosemary, cinnamon, or thyme

Tealights

Cornucopia basket (woven or made from wire-shaped burlap and raffia ropes)

Feast foods for the cornucopia basket (see below)

3 empty baskets

To the ancient pagans, the Second Harvest was a time to express gratitude for the abundance of the season as well as each other as they headed into the darkness together. They held a great feast, at the center of which was a cornucopia to represent the Earth's bounty. There are many folk stories about the origin of the cornucopia, and the Greek tale of Zeus has an interesting spin on the "horn of plenty." According to legend, baby Zeus was hidden deep in a cave and nursed to health by the tender goat goddess, Amaltheia. Not knowing his own strength, Zeus accidentally broke off the goat's horn, after which it provided eternal nourishment. In a symbolic gesture to its mystical origins, the goat horn was filled with seasonal feast foods such as fruits, vegetables, grains, and nuts during the pagan Thanksgiving.

Lay an altar cloth in the colors of the Second Harvest on the feast table and decorate it with autumn leaves and dried corn cobs. Hollow out the centers of self-standing gourds and brush the insides with an anointing oil made from botanically infused olive oil. Place tealights inside them. Herbs such as sage, rosemary, cinnamon, and thyme will release their scent as tealights warm the inside of the gourds. In the center of the altar cloth, place the cornucopia basket. Fill the cornucopia with the bounty of the Second Harvest: gourds, apples, pomegranates, grapes, carrots, potatoes, onions, corn, figs, hearty breads made with herbs, pumpkin and butternut squash soups, sweet potato dishes, pies, a jug of wine decorated with grape bunches and vines, and the like. Next to it, place one basket for collecting nonperishable items to donate to a food drive or pantry, another to collect fruit and vegetables for wildlife, and a third for offerings to the gods and goddesses of Mabon if deities are in your practice.

CORNER OF GRATITUDE

Express your gratitude for the abundance of the season.

Materials

Wooden round

Fireproof pot

Mini pumpkins, gourds, apples, or other symbols of the harvest

Orange crystals such as carnelian and orange calcite, or gratitude and abundance crystals such as green aventurine and tiger's eye

Palm-sized stone (optional)

Small bowl of bay leaves and a pen

During this season of thanks, gratitude is given to the Sun, the land, and our loved ones for all that has prepared us for the difficult months ahead. But what about gratitude for ourselves? When we honor the work that we have done, we not only instill confidence and pride in ourselves, but we take stock of all that we have left to do. Mabon is a season of balance—of harvest, yes, but also of repose—a time to visualize not only the fruits of our labor, but what preparations we might have missed. How well did our intentions grow? Did we receive the bounty we had hoped for? Do we have everything we need to carry us through the dark days ahead?

Create this altar in a corner of your home or in the hollow of a tree along a wooded path. On a stump or a wooden round, place a fireproof pot. Decorate the base of the pot with mini pumpkins, gourds, apples, or other symbols of the harvest. Include orange crystals such as carnelian and orange calcite or crystals for gratitude and abundance such as green aventurine and tiger's eye. If you like, create a gratitude stone by charging a palm-sized stone with everything for which you are thankful. Next to the pot, place a small bowl of bay leaves. On the leaves, write notes of gratitude for each of your intentions that has come to fruition during the Second Harvest. Use the stones to charge the notes before you place them in the pot. Next, write down any intentions that still have room for growth, and set them aside to revisit during the Third Harvest. At the end of your ritual, set fire to the notes in the pot, and blow the ashes into the wind to spread your gratitude over the land and its creatures.

Note: *This altar can double as an offering to the wildlife, who are also busily preparing for the cold months ahead.*

APPLE DIVINATION ALTAR

Divine matters of the heart with the sacred knowledge of apples.

Materials

Black altar cloth

Small, round table

Bowl of freshly harvested apples

Knife

2 black taper candles

Apple blossom incense

Incense burner

The apple has long been considered a sacred source of wisdom. During the harvest season, apple divination is often employed to foretell matters of the heart. In ancient Rome, apple seeds were thrown into the fire. A loud pop meant that the person the thrower loved would love them back. In English and Irish folklore, if a woman peeled an apple in one continuous peel and threw it over her shoulder, it would land in the shape of her true love's initials. Another English folk tradition says that if you squeeze a seed between your fingers so that the pippin flies out, it will fly in the direction of the home of your one true love. T. F. Thiselton-Dyer includes a little apple charm for this divination method in his 1889 book, *The Folk-Lore of Plants*:

Pippin, pippin paradise,
Tell me M'here niy true love lies,
East, west, north, and south.
Pilling Brig, or Cocker mouth.

Romani legend has it that if a maiden buys an apple from a widow on Saint Andrew's Eve on November 29, she can eat half before midnight and the other half after midnight to dream of her future husband.

Place a black altar cloth down on a small, round table in a room that is bathed in the illumination of the Full Harvest Moon. Fashion a pair of apple candleholders by carving out the tops of each apple and inserting black candles for protection against negative energies. In an incense burner, burn apple blossom incense to drive away ill-intentioned spirits and increase psychic ability. To call upon the spirit element, slice an apple in half horizontally to display the pentagram of seeds, and place it on the altar. In the center of the altar, place a bowl of freshly harvested apples and a knife. Although crabapples are thought to hold the most power for divination, any variety of apple will do. Use the altar when trying any apple divination method.

SCALES OF EQUALITY

Bring your whole self into perfect balance.

Materials

Black altar cloth that has been painted or embroidered with a white pentacle, a triskele, or another symbol that represents death and rebirth

Balance scales (or a set crafted from an old wooden hanger, string or twine, and two tin pails or hanging planters)

Tumbled obsidian and clear quartz pieces, all of approximately the same size and weight

2 bowls

Incense burner

Calming incense such as sandalwood, chamomile, or lavender

During Mabon, Dark Mother energy abounds, signaling the impending death of the land as the light hangs precariously above us. Much like the Vernal Equinox, the Autumnal Equinox is the perfect time to illuminate and transform all that hinders you. The seeds that have been buried deep in our psyche out of conditioning, fear, or trauma must be allowed to grow into healthy thoughts and habits. Addressing our shadow self head-on and working to shift patterns can help us to grow even in the dormant time.

This altar will act as a sacred space in which to visualize your whole self in perfect balance. On a solid, steady surface in a quiet room, place a black altar cloth that has been painted or embroidered with a white pentacle, a triskele, or another symbol that represents death and rebirth. In the center, place a set of balance scales or suspend it from a plant hook above your altar. Place obsidian tumbles in a bowl; obsidian is known to break down barriers, cutting to the heart of the matter and revealing the shadow self. Place clear quartz tumbles in another bowl; clear quartz is known to bring light to a situation and to transform negative energy. In an incense burner, burn incense such as sandalwood, chamomile, or lavender to ease the anxiety that often results from a deep dive into your psyche. Think of this altar as a place where you will symbolically balance your shadow self with the stones. As you try to find two stones of equal weight, visualize the obsidian as an unearthed shadow that you are bringing into the light to transform. Once you find the clear quartz balance stone, it has been done.

BEDSIDE DREAM TRAY

Encourage protected, but productive dreams.

Materials

Silver tray or dish

Purple altar cloth

Bundle of lavender or natural fiber dream pillow containing apple seeds, dried apple blossoms, lavender, and sage

Dream ointment or oil: evening primrose oil infused with mugwort, lavender, and wormwood

Dream crystals such as amethyst, selenite, and celestite

Purple candle

Bell

Traditional dreamcatcher made by an Ojibwa artisan (optional)

Mabon is the threshold of autumn, the time of the year when the leaves turn vibrant shades of color on their descent into decay. Although light and dark balance on the equinox scale, there comes a tipping point. As Samhain nears, the veil between our world and the spirit world becomes easily traversed. Negative energies cross, sometimes taking hold of our dreams and turning them into nightmares. For this, we must prepare. Even in rest, we cannot play to the shadows in the absence of light.

To ensure that your sleep is productive and protected even on the precipice of darkness, prepare a bedside tray for dream rituals. On a silver tray or dish, lay an altar cloth in purple, the color of spiritual ascension. Include a bundle of lavender or a dream pillow made from a natural fiber sachet containing apple seeds, dried apple blossoms, lavender, and sage to place over your eyes or under your pillow. Create an anointing oil or ointment made from evening primrose oil infused with mugwort, lavender, and wormwood and place it on the tray. This can be massaged into the space between your eyebrows to assist in opening your third eye. Include crystals known to assist with lucid dreaming and astral travel, such as amethyst, selenite, and celestite. A single purple candle can be used as a focal point as you drift into the dream realm. Include a bell to call yourself back and scare away spirits or negative energies that might linger before or after your ritual. If you can purchase a traditional dreamcatcher from a member of the Ojibwa (Chippewa) tribe, the Native American originators of the dreamcatcher, you may hang it above your bed. These authentic Native American dreamcatchers are typically woven of willow and sinew and finished with feathers and nettle. They were originally created by Ojibwe grandparents to hang over the cradles of infants to filter bad dreams while they slept.

CHAPTER 8

SAMHAIN

Northern Hemisphere: October 31; Southern Hemisphere: April 31

On the old Irish calendar, Samhain brought the death of the Sun and the descent into darkness. As the last harvest festival on the Wheel of the Year, it ushers people in from the cold, barren fields to the comfort of their hearths and homes. Like Beltane, Samhain is a liminal time when the veil between this world and the next is thin. The ancient Celts believed that the Sun descended into the otherworld and that Donn, the Lord of the Dead in Celtic mythology, roamed the Earth with his fellow spectral denizens. Ghostly legends, faeries, and reanimated corpses were all thought to walk amongst the living on Samhain—an event for which the ancient pagans prepared. Many enduring traditions evolved from this fear and focused on the protection of homes, fields, and people against troublesome Samhain spirits. In rural regions, bonfires were lit in the farm fields to shield stored crops and livestock from witches. Spooky jack-o'-lanterns decorated the porches and scary costumes were donned to confuse the spirits. The Celts were also sure to appease their own dead in hopes that they would receive their wisdom and blessings for the coming season.

Modern pagan celebrations have reconstructed many of the ancient Samhain traditions, with a focus on ancestor veneration, divination, and spirit communication. Celtic-influenced "Witches' Balls" are often held at this time so that the living may dance and imbibe with the spirits who mingle among them. Halloween, the popular western holiday on the eve of the Christian feast of All Hallows' Day, is thought to have evolved from Samhain. Much like many of the pagan holidays on the Wheel of the Year, Samhain was not a festival the ancient pagans were willing to forgo upon conversion to Christianity. Trick-or-treating, mumming, pumpkin carving, apple bobbing, and ghostly legends are all traditions that have endured thousands of years of roving ideologies

SAMHAIN ALTAR

The Samhain altar embraces the shadows as the Sun finally makes its descent into darkness. It is an altar of reverence, a place to consider what will be coming to an end and what will guide you through winter. It will also be a working altar, and it should have its own place beside the feast table or in the gathering room.

MAGICKAL CORRESPONDENCES OF SAMHAIN

ALTERNATIVE NAMES: Third Harvest, All Hallows' Eve (Christian), Hallowmas (Celtic/Scottish)

COLORS: Orange, black, white, silver

CRYSTALS: Black tourmaline, obsidian, jet, onyx, smoky quartz, hematite, howlite, labradorite, garnet, ruby, amber, petrified wood

DEITIES: Anubis (Egyptian), the Morrigan (Celtic), Hel (Norse), Hades (Greek), Donn (Celtic)

ELEMENT: Water/Earth

FLOWERS, HERBS, AND TREES: Rosemary, blessed thistle, nutmeg, clove, cinnamon, sage, angelica, orange, mugwort, mullein, myrrh, patchouli

FOODS: Pumpkins, gourds, candied apples, gingerbread, candy, cakes, barmbrack, colcannon, wine, cider

SYMBOLS: Jack-o'-lanterns, bonfires, autumn leaves, apples, skulls, acorns, besom, cauldron

THEMES: Harvest, divination, ancestor veneration, spirit communication, death

To draw the magick of the Moon to the altar, locate it in a room that is in full view of the moonlight via a window or skylight. On the surface of the altar, lay white gauze or lace over a black cloth to represent the thinning veil. You may even want to lay down an actual veil that has been passed down to you through the generations. Feel free to have a bit of fun with this altar and incorporate Halloween traditions as well—fabric decorated in pumpkins, black cats, bats, or witches can be a festive addition to the Samhain altar. Decorate the altar with symbols of the afterlife, such as skulls, bones, ashes, urns, ghostly portraits, a scythe, the Death tarot card, or grave rubbings of your ancestors' stones.

The lights on Samhain serve a dual purpose: Not only do they guide your ancestors home as they make the long journey from the veil, but they ward off any negative energies that might take advantage of this liminal time. Lanterns, candles, jack-o'-lanterns, and string lights can all offer a protected path. You may also want to include a wand or a ceremonial Wiccan blade known as an athame for directing light to the altar or for casting energies away after you have completed your divination and spirit communication rituals.

Flowers and herbs that are deep and rich in color can bring the Samhain season indoors to your altar. If you like, preserve or dry the flowers a few weeks before Samhain so that they may represent the dormancy of life even in darkness. Dried autumn leaves, black, purple, or orange irises, roses, lilies, carnations, marigolds, chrysanthemums, rosemary, sage, mugwort, and thyme can be placed in vases, empty urns, or hung on the walls or ceilings above the altar. Crops from the Third Harvest are also an excellent addition to the Samhain altar. Pumpkins, gourds,

The Samhain altar embraces the shadows as the Sun finally makes its descent into darkness. It is an altar of reverence, a place to consider what will be coming to an end and what will guide you through winter.

apples, and grains can be made into candle holders or carved with symbols of protection such as Algiz, the Elder Futhark rune of protection. Include a besom made from willow or apple tree twigs and dust it with spices of the season, such as cinnamon, nutmeg, and clove, so that you can symbolically sweep away any negative energy that might enter your home.

Elementally, Samhain begins the transition from the emotional balancing act of Water to the grounding stability of Earth. If you like, represent this new energy with a bowl of graveyard dirt, soil, or salt in the northern quarter of your altar. The other elements can be represented by placing symbols of the season in their respective directions: incense of dragon's blood, cinnamon, or cloves in the southern direction of Fire, a raven or crow feather in the eastern direction of Air, and a cauldron in the western direction of Water. By calling each element in balance to our sacred space, we invite the ascended Spirit energy into the Samhain altar. This energetic space is where the spirits speak.

The liminal festival of Samhain is the opportune time to practice your divination skills. The divination section of your main altar will be an active area and can include tools that you feel comfortable working with: for example, scrying mirrors, crystal balls, tarot cards, dowsing pendulums, spirit boards, or runes. Include an herbal spray or anointing oil crafted from a mugwort, wormwood, and yarrow infusion as well as amethyst or ruby in fuchsite for opening your third eye. For protection against negative entities or unwanted energies, combine cleansing and protective herbs

By calling each element in balance to our sacred space, we invite the ascended Spirit energy into the Samhain altar. This energetic space is where the spirits speak.

such as sage and cedar with Witches' Black Salt (see page 43) and cast a circle around your divination tools. Black tourmaline, obsidian, and onyx can add an extra level of protection to your altar. You may also have a bottle of sacred water that you have infused with cedar, sage, or rue to sprinkle around the altar to dispel negative energies before you begin divination of spirit communication work.

Although you may have a separate ancestor shrine to honor your loved ones that have passed, including a few ancestor photos or mementos on the main altar can help to call their energy to your divination practice. In lieu of photos, you might carve each of your ancestors' names on white taper candles and arrange them according to the family tree in a candelabra.

JACK-O'-LANTERN WARD

Protect your home against unwanted energies.

Materials

Pumpkins, gourds, or other root vegetables

Apple or small pumpkin for incense

Knife

Scoop

Tealights

Protection incense such as sage, cedarwood, frankincense, sandalwood, or cinnamon

Offering plate of food and drink (optional)

While the fragile Samhain veil allows well-meaning ancestors to come home to their families, it also opens the gate for other types of spirits to cross into the Earthly realm. The faerie folk prance around, pulling pranks on unsuspecting humans, and the evil spirits of the otherworld exact revenge on those they seek. In ancient Ireland, turnips, rutabagas, gourds, beets, and potatoes were carved with heinous grins and lit with embers to ward off evil spirits. Irish folklore tells the story of "Stingy Jack," a trickster who was admitted entrance to neither heaven nor hell but was given an ember by the Devil to light his way out of the Netherworld. He placed this ember in a turnip and eternally roamed the Earth with his "jack-o'-lantern." When early Irish immigrants arrived in North America, they held on to this tradition, but substituted the widely grown pumpkin for the turnip.

Carve pumpkins, gourds, or other root vegetables into "jack-o'-lanterns" to not only guide your ancestors on their way home, but to protect your home from wandering, baneful energies. To do this, carefully cut off the top with a knife, then scoop out the insides with a scoop, thoroughly scraping the sides. Finally, use the knife to cut the expressive face of your choice into the side. Place a tealight inside each jack-o'-lantern you carve. Place the jack-o'-lanterns just outside your entry, on a porch or stoop, facing the road or path to your home. Inside of a hollowed apple or pumpkin, burn incense known to offer protection against negative energies. You may also want to place a smaller altar with offerings of food and drink to the spirits in the West—the direction where spirits are thought to dwell in the afterlife. Here, traveling spirits with no family can be appeased, particularly if you are living in their old home that they wish to visit. At each quarter around your home, bury apples that have been enchanted with a warding spell, for example, "Protect my home and spirit from those who wish them harm."

SPIRIT FEAST TABLE

Invite welcome spirits to your Samhain feast.

Materials

Black lace or tulle

White tablecloth

Vase of dried flowers

Black tourmaline sphere

Candelabra (optional)

Black or white dinnerware

Tealight

Sage or cedar bundle

Samhain feast food: mulled wine and cider, dark breads, soul cakes, hearty stews and soups, pumpkin pie, spiced cakes and cookies, colcannon, and barmbrack

Food made from an ancestors' recipe (optional)

As the third and final harvest festival on the Wheel of the Year, Samhain celebrates the food crops that ripen just before the winter winds rip across the barren fields. Corn, pumpkins, gourds, squash, apples, pomegranates, root vegetables such as turnips and beets, potatoes, and nuts and seeds are all reaped from the fields in one final effort to prepare for the dark days ahead. Whatever cannot be harvested by sunset is left in the fields, an offering to the spirits that wander across the veil to their Earthly abodes. As they make their way home, they follow the path we have lit for them, stopping every so often to partake in the remnants of the harvest. When they finally arrive home, they will be expecting a warm and cozy seat at their family's feast table, complete with their favorite foods and perhaps a glass of wine or a pint of ale. The "Dumb Supper" of Samhain is a feast for the living and the dead alike. It was originally a meal consumed in complete silence—in this case "dumb" meant mute—and operated similarly to a seance. There is anecdotal evidence that Victorian era dumb suppers were often held for divination purposes. At midnight, women who wished to know the identity of their future husbands would lay out a meal in a backward fashion, perhaps in a spooky, abandoned house, in hopes that the spirits

> *The "Dumb Supper" of Samhain is a feast for the living and the dead alike. It was originally a meal consumed in complete silence—in this case "dumb" meant mute—and operated similarly to a seance.*

of their future lovers would join them. The Ozarks, too, seem to have been a powerful place for the tradition of dumb suppers. In the 1920 book *Kentucky Superstitions*, Daniel L. and Lucy B. Thomas wrote:

"Silent supper." Several girls make a fire and prepare a supper together, not speaking, and always walking backwards. They place a pan of water on the doorstep and hang a towel near, They sit at the table but do not eat anything. If these conditions are observed, the future husbands of the girls will come, wash, sit opposite them, and finally disappear.

Another passage explains:

A deaf and dumb supper is prepared as follows. While preparing this supper the participants must neither speak or be spoken to by any one. All the work must be done backwards, that is, they walk backwards and hold hands behind them while doing the work. When all is ready for eating, some supernatural sign appears to them. Sometimes it is two men carrying a corpse; or a large white dog may appear. Whatever it may be, it is always very alarming in appearance.

In modern Samhain celebrations, this traditional dumb supper has evolved into a time to appease our dead with offerings and to listen for the whispers of their spirits. On a dining table, lay down black lace or tulle over a white tablecloth. Place a vase of dried flowers in the center of the table along with a sphere of black tourmaline for radiating protective energies. If you like, include a candelabra in the centerpiece; each candle represents one of your ancestors. You may use the same candles from your main Samhain altar and carry them ceremoniously into the dining area. Set the table with black or white dinnerware, leaving a place setting for your ancestors at the head of the table. If you have space to place a setting for each of your ancestors individually, you may do so, but it is not necessary. On their plate, place a tealight to guide them to their seat. Before your guests arrive, cleanse the energy of the room with sage or cedar smoke and cast a circle of protection around the table. The dumb

In modern Samhain celebrations, this traditional dumb supper has evolved into a time to appease our dead with offerings and to listen for the whispers of their spirits.

supper can include dishes made from late harvest foods such as mulled wine and cider, dark breads, "soul cakes" (a Christian cake to commemorate the dead on All Souls' Day), hearty stews and soups, pumpkin pie, spiced cakes and cookies, and the traditional Irish foods of colcannon and barmbrack. You may also want to try an old recipe from a family member who has passed and present this at the spirit feast. In the traditional English way, you may also want to serve the supper entirely backward with dessert first followed by the meal and then the appetizer. As you dish out the food, remember to serve it to your ancestor's plate as well. Include a gracious pour of their favorite wine, ale, or liquor. Most importantly, remember not to speak or the whispers of your ancestors might not be heard. On their way out of the dining area, guests may leave a token of remembrance at the main altar or ancestor shrine.

ANCESTOR SHRINE

Honor those in your family who have passed.

Materials

Altar cloth, such as antique piece of lace or blanket

Family tree

Picture frame

Ancestor mementos and photos

Dried flowers and ancestral crystals such as petrified wood and amber

White candles

Ancestor mementos

Ancestor money (optional)

Fireproof vessel (optional)

Mugwort and cedar (optional)

At sunset on Samhain, the Celtic New Year begins and our ancestors make their way over from the afterlife. They come expecting gracious hospitality after their arduous journey and take their seat at the dumb supper to indulge in their favorite Earthly delights. After supper, everyone gathers 'round the fire to chat. Family members inform the dead of the news and gossip since their last visit during Beltane. We do this not only to keep the memories of our loved ones alive, but to earn their guidance and wisdom from the spiritual realm.

Create this altar in a room where guests will gather after the dumb supper. The table itself could be a family heirloom, perhaps passed down by one of your visiting ancestors. The altar cloth, too, could be an antique piece of lace or a blanket. Print out or draw your family tree, inserting photos where you can, and place it in a frame at the center of the altar. Decorate the altar with dried flowers and ancestral crystals such as petrified wood and amber. Assign each ancestor their own space on the altar and include mementos from their lives or a few of their favorite pastimes, such as food, liquor, cigars, flowers, perfume, clothing, or jewelry. Include a white candle at each space and ensure the candles remain lit throughout the evening. If you like, you may also engage in the Chinese tradition of burning "ancestor money" at the altar. Burning this faux money—also known as spirit or ghost money, joss paper, or hell notes—is thought to send real money to your dearly departed in the afterlife. It is often offered in enormous sums so that you ancestors will be well taken care of in the spirit world. After folding the money, you may light it on fire it at each respective candle, allowing it to burn in a central fireproof vessel on a bed of mugwort and cedar.

DIVINATION TRAVEL TIN

Hone your divination craft even while on the go.

Materials

Hinged or lidded tin

Moss or dried herbs such as sage and mugwort

Selenite wand

Divination crystal such as amethyst, labradorite, or celestite

Protection crystals such as black tourmaline and obsidian

Divination tools

Divination has been a part of Samhain since ancient times. During this liminal time, not only can spirits cross over to pass on knowledge from the otherworld, but we can cross over to glean the information ourselves. Ancient pagan divination practices during Samhain included bonfire rites and games that would foretell the growth of crops and romantic interests of the villagers. The Irish tea cake, barmbrack, was traditionally filled with a set of symbolic objects such as a coin for wealth, a button for eternal bachelorhood, a thimble for spinsterhood, a key for a journey, and a piece of cloth for poverty. The object embedded in your piece of cake indicated your future.

Modern divination often goes beyond the predictions of the ancient pagans. Tarot cards, dowsing pendulums, runes, crystal balls, scrying mirrors, and bone casting can all be used to communicate with our ancestors as they guide us along uncertain paths. Even if you are traveling and cannot partake in the Samhain feast or ancestor altar, a divination tin can be taken on the go to communicate with the spirit world. Line a hinged or lidded tin with a bed of moss or dried herbs such as sage and mugwort. Include a selenite wand for cleansing the room's energy. You may also want to include a small crystal to aid in opening the channels of communication: amethyst, labradorite, or celestite are all excellent crystal allies to have on hand for divination purposes. Protection, too, will be of utmost importance given the strange and unusual energies you might encounter—black tourmaline and obsidian act as your shields, absorbing and transforming negative energy. Finally, decide which divination method you would prefer to take on the road. If you choose to include a dowsing pendulum, you can paste a small dowsing board on the lid of the tin. There are even pocket-sized tarot decks that can give you full-size readings during your travels in this life and the next.

ACKNOWLEDGMENTS

Once again, I must first and foremost send blessings to my circle, the online witching community, for all of the incredible inspiration, support, and sense of community that they have provided. The energy they radiate, even through virtual channels, is palpable. My son, of course, is always a source of deep inspiration along with my husband, parents, brother, and family. My beautiful friends Becki and Meaghan . . . where would I be without your honest but loving support? And finally, without the expertise and investment of the following people at Fair Winds Press, this book would have been nothing more than ideas floating in the air: Thank you to Jill for being the best editor without whom I would be directionless, John for guiding me effortlessly through the editing and design process, Tiffany and Elizabeth for their insightful editing, Anne for another round of incredible art vision and direction, the design team for the beauty in the pages, Lydia in marketing for believing in my work, and the entire team at Fair Winds Press for the opportunity to share the most beloved aspect of my life.

To the ancestors that have paved our paths and still light my way, I owe my eternal gratitude.

ABOUT THE AUTHOR

Since the mid-1990s, Anjou has sought the magick that resides within us and the natural world. At an early age, she toiled in potions and herbal remedies, explored tarot and the realm of spirits, and began a lifelong grimoire that would ultimately lead her down the path of sharing her craft with the community. From her childhood spent in the woods and later settling on a magickally-minded homestead in the rolling hills of rural Maine, she has cultivated a craft based on her own observations of nature and continued her spiritual journey through the hedges. Named as one of Refinery29's "Magical Women on Instagram You Really Should be Following," Anjou thrives on sharing her lifelong exploration of witchcraft and cultivation of magickal spaces.

Anjou holds a bachelor's of arts in biology with a minor in anthropology and has enjoyed many extracurricular courses in history, art, ecology, botany, herbalism, and literature. She enjoys painting, writing, gardening, reading, antiquing, conserving and exploring nature, and being a mama to the most magickal little boy.

INDEX